Get Your Free Gift!

Whilst understanding the context of this
feeling of it. Whilst learning takes place
very helpful to see how the movements ⌐
Therefore, to get the best experience with this book, here is a link for you to
access a free 20-minute guided video of some of the movements you'll find
explained in part 2. I've found that readers who download and use this video
are more effective at releasing tension, and as a result are better able to create
more comfort and freedom in how they move and feel.

So go ahead and access your own free 20-minute video to get started. You can
get a copy by visiting:

www.somatichabit.co.uk/freeclass

And for more information you can also head to:

www.somatichabit.co.uk

SOMATIC
movement

SOMATIC
movement

Restoring functional, pain-free movement and moving towards connection and wholeness

KAREN STATNER

For more information, email contact@somatichabit.co.uk
ISBN: 979-8-89109-678-3 (paperback)
ISBN: 979-8-89109-679-0 (ebook)

ABOUT THE AUTHOR

Karen lives in the beautiful historic city of York from where she founded and runs her business Somatic Habit™. She runs weekly zoom and studio classes, clinical sessions and offers an online membership. She has been teaching and sharing her love of clinical somatic education since 2016 and certified as a Clinical Somatic Educator in 2022. She undertook her training with Essential Somatics™ and is now part of this highly skilled and experienced training team, running workshops and helping to train and mentor the next generation of Essential Somatic movement teachers. As well as her love for all things somatics, she loves walking in the mountains, climbing, festivals, exploring new lands and cozy nights in. At the root of her teachings is her belief that all of us, no matter our age, background, or experiences, have the ability to create more space and freedom in how we function and live.

This book is dedicated
to
all freedom and autonomy-seeking somas

TABLE OF CONTENTS

FOREWORD

Hanna Somatic Education refers to the work based upon the late Dr. Thomas Hanna, a somatic pioneer who set up the Novato Institute (www.somaticsed. com/novlnstitute.html). He also referred to his work as Clinical Somatic Education. Tragically, he died as a result of a car accident in the early 1990s. This happened before he had fully completed the clinical training to his first group of students. I can just imagine how their teacher's death may have, to some extent, taken the wind out of their sails. Fortunately for us, these students continued to take his work forward despite him suddenly being gone from their lives. I can only imagine the effort this must have taken, as well as the strength and depth of belief in what they had learnt from Hanna up to that point. Fast forward some years, and Essential Somatics™ (www.essentialsomatics.com), founded by Martha Peterson has continued to build upon Hanna's work and spreads this throughout the world. I completed my movement teacher training and clinical somatic education (CSE) training with Essential Somatics™, which is the one-to-one and hands-on element of Hanna's work.

The terms Hanna Somatic Education (HSE) and Clinical Somatic Education (CSE) are interchangeable, and Hanna used both terms when talking about his work. For the sake of consistency, I shall refer to Hanna's work and the evolution of this through Essential Somatics™ as Clinical Somatic Education (CSE). In using this term, I am referring to your own somatic movement practise, that which you'd experience in joining a group movement class, and the one-to-one clinical hands-on work. Where I refer to the term "somatics" in a more general sense or in reference to other modalities, I hope to make that clear to you.

You may have noticed that the term "somatics" is becoming more widely used and recognised. Therefore, before taking you any further, I would like to clarify what this means and, specifically, what I mean by this term and how I use it throughout this book. The word "somatics" comes from the Greek word *soma*, meaning living body experienced from within. Considering and experiencing oneself as a soma, a whole living system from within, is profoundly different to viewing oneself as a body with parts. The general use of the word "somatics" can be understood as an umbrella term, under which different somatic modalities focus upon the field of internal awareness and the felt sense as experienced from within. You may already have come across or heard of other somatic methods and somatic pioneers prior to Hanna. Those who seem to be most well known are F. M. Alexander, who developed The Alexander Technique, and Moshe Feldenkrais with his method of Awareness Through Movement.

To support you in your learning, this book is made up of two parts. The first part explores what this method is and dips a toe into exploring the science that underpins this work and how it differs from other methods. Despite the life-changing and profound impact that can be experienced through Hanna Somatic Education, it isn't magic or "woo woo." This work is rooted in our neurophysiology and only possible because of our continued ability to learn, thanks to neuroplasticity. It isn't magic; it's deliberate, intentional, and specific, with its foundations rooted in science. In Part 1 of this book I'll also take you through the context in which Hanna Somatic Education sits. Exploring the context is as necessary as exploring the science. If we're to understand ourselves and move towards spaciousness, freedom, and autonomy, we must consider the context in which we live, and the essence of who we are. Exploring the context of this method opens up discussion and consideration of how we live as somas, meaning, a living body experienced from within. We can begin to explore how our lived experience manifests and the cultural and lifestyle consequences for all of us in how we feel, move, and live. As I find myself saying often, this is so much more than just movement.

Having set the scene in Part 1, the second part will guide you through how to do specific Hanna somatic movements, helping you to begin your own practice for restoring functional and pain-free movement. Part 2 will also guide you through daily sequences, how you can create a regular somatic movement habit for yourself, and next steps.

By writing this book, I share with you my learnings and observations of the power of this work for myself and what I've been fortunate to witness take place for others. My experience of doing this has been and continues to be a humbling experience. As well as sharing what I've learnt, I also write about the innumerable ways in which this work connects to and embeds within all aspects of our lives. I share the aspects of our culture and reference other available knowledge and understanding that interests me and which I believe to be of relevance to this work. In my experience so far, the work of those whom I reference throughout, combined with my personal somatic education have helped me to continue growing, questioning, and being ever curious in the pursuit of function, freedom, and autonomy. To write this book for you has been a joyful indulgence. Thank you for being here; now let's get started!

PART 1

CHAPTER 1

Introduction

It's May bank holiday 2006. I'm in York District Hospital, lying in a bed and overhearing a consultant refer to me as "the girl with the back." I remember thinking, *Are there people out there without backs?* It had been a few days since my riding accident, in which I'd done my best superhero impersonation of flying through the air from horseback and landing some distance away in a field. Things had not gone as planned! Fortunately, my friend's horse, which, ideally, I would still have been sitting on, was fine. I, on the other hand, now had a broken back.

A few days later, my back brace had been fitted, and it was time to get vertical. With my shoulders hitched up around my ears and my torso fixed in place thanks to my new shiny brace accessory, I did my best robot walk up and down the ward, imitating a walking fridge freezer with arms and legs. I was supported in my new robot walk by a physiotherapist who told me that when the time came it would be essential that I do Pilates to *strengthen my core* as part of my rehabilitation. "Strengthen your core" was a phrase I was to become very familiar with. Interestingly, the word rehabilitation comes from the Latin word *habilis*, meaning "to make fit, to make able." Not that making myself "fit" or "able" in this sense was the path that I initially went down, but what could be more *fitting* than to restore functional movement *before* strengthening and tightening? I digress; back to 2006! After a few months, I had a memorable appointment with a consultant, who somewhat sternly asked me if I knew how fortunate I was. He then proceeded to paint a rather detailed picture of what was waiting for me. He described an image of a very frail and "elderly" woman, unable to stand upright, bent over, and walking with a stick. In his candid and matter-of-fact tone, he proceeded to tell me that this image is how I would be, just a lot sooner than most folks. *"You cannot be serious!"* I screamed silently in my head. This was not music to my 26-year-old ears, so like an obedient and somewhat now terrified patient, I did my physio sessions and homework. Then months later, when I'd been given the all clear, I took my first Pilates class and started work to strengthen my core.

Pilates was a completely new experience for me, and it had a big impact upon my life; I even went on to teach it. For someone who wasn't particularly sporty and hadn't done exercise like this before, that was a big step outside of my comfort zone. However, obstacles along this path were raising doubts about the effectiveness of what I was repeatedly doing and teaching. Thanks to my ongoing confusion and frustration in how I felt and moved, I couldn't shake off the questions that I had around recurring niggles, pain, and restricted movement. These sensations were ongoing and, at times, getting worse, despite having worked hard to *strengthen my core*. I didn't understand what I was feeling or why. I was also becoming increasingly annoyed about how I'd become dependent upon massages and needing the next one only a few weeks after the last one had "reset" and put me right. This felt like a path away from freedom and autonomy and towards dependency and a lower bank balance, neither of which I was feeling good about.

Then, into my life came the method of movement education developed by Dr. Thomas Hanna; a deliberate and intentional method of somatic movement to restore functional and pain-free movement. To describe somatics as being the missing piece of the puzzle is to put it very mildly. The more I dipped my toes into this method, the more I came to understand what I was feeling and why. I began to better understand what was contributing to my recurring back pain, always on one side, why I was looking increasingly lopsided in photos and why back extension exercises felt horrid. Somatics cracked open a door through which I began to explore and better understand why continuing to work at *strengthening my core* in the way that I was, was leading me towards more pain. This new learning was blowing my mind; I was learning how to finally relieve and even reverse these discomforts and misalignments. After years of being and feeling dependent upon others to "put me right" and feel relief, this really was profound. The clouds were parting, and I was becoming clearer and feeling more connected and empowered than ever. These changes were taking place because I was no longer focusing on and trying to treat the symptoms, the standard approach to health, deeply reinforced through Western culture. Rather, I was heading to the causes, compensations, and holding patterns that were underlying those symptoms. Treating symptoms is always going to be a short-term "fix." What symptoms can offer us, though, are doorways and signposts towards the causes, our unconscious patterns and habits. Addressing and affecting the causes is where the long-term changes take place. Whilst this may sound simple enough, the process of becoming aware of the underlying causes of my symptoms wasn't clear-cut from the start; in fact, it was far from it for me. My initial experiences of somatic movement left me more confused. How could I not feel the smallest and seemingly simplest of functional movements when I'd been diligently practicing Pilates for years by this point? I knew then that I had so much yet to learn and was becoming ever more aware of how much I didn't know. I knew that I needed time to explore what I could learn from my confusion and, at times, frustration. I knew I was missing or lacking in something; I just didn't know what it was, but oh how I wanted and needed to find out. My spark of curiosity had well and truly been lit and was growing!

As I continued my somatic explorations and learning, my pain was reducing, and my range of comfortable movement was increasing. I felt I was moving away from prematurely becoming that bent-over frail lady walking with a stick; great! But this is only part of my experience that keeps unfolding and evolving. What I find so fascinating about this method and what keeps me coming back for more, is the awareness it gives me, how it helps me to be present and continue moving towards space, freedom, and autonomy.

I had been attributing my niggles, inner tension, functioning and holding patterns to that one isolated riding accident because I believed that nothing so significant had happened before in my life. I held it as a fundamental aspect of my identity. My physical injury was indeed a catalyst for change and finding somatics. However, by narrowing my story and focusing upon my injury, I had completely written off and disregarded the accumulation and impact of my 26 years of life before that point. I had disregarded, or perhaps never really recognised, how my experiences of life had accumulated and manifested in my nervous system. I had neither appreciated nor understood how my perspectives, decisions, and connection with others, especially with myself, had been so deeply influenced by those prior 26 years. This was all showing up as areas of discomfort, pain, and symptoms such as IBS, conflict, coping mechanisms, even my personality. What I have come to learn through somatics is that the accumulation of how I had lived my life before and since my accident was absolutely embedded within my nervous system. This accumulation affects every aspect of my being, whether I'm consciously aware of it or not. Becoming more aware of how our life creates a "layered presence," as Hanna described it, is fundamental to understanding how we feel, function, and live. From this awareness and the questions and curiosity that follow, opportunities for creating long-term changes can occur. I shall talk more about this area later on, particularly in Chapter 9, where I'll take you through the fundamental role that somatics plays in healing and moving towards wholeness.

You probably have one or several reasons for picking up this book. My reason for writing it is to help continue spreading this necessary and much needed work. My intention is to make this method of movement education increasingly accessible, so that we may all have opportunities for exploring our own somatic process and move towards creating more space, freedom, and connection for ourselves, if we choose. I'm not inventing the wheel here; rather, I hope to do justice to and uphold the powerful and profound work and knowledge that others have laid before me. I'm deeply grateful and indebted to them for sharing this work, which has profoundly changed my life. This knowledge and learning that I have received isn't mine to keep or own, rather it's my responsibility to share to the best of my ability and with integrity, with those willing and interested to listen. Passing that forward, I hope I can support you in learning and creating change for yourself. May this book be a source of clarity and integrity along your way.

Through reading and engaging with this book, may you begin to explore your own somatic process with compassion and curiosity. May it support you in becoming more aware of the impact of your life and to move towards living more comfortably, whatever that looks like for you and from wherever your starting point is. This is a handbook to guide you towards your own somatic habit. If, like me, you're not averse to scribbling, underlining, and highlighting parts that challenge or resonate, I encourage you to engage with this by making notes and writing answers to the questions that I pose throughout. Engaging in what you read in this way helps to expand and deepen your learning. If you'd rather not write in your book, I recommend having a place to record your reflections, observations, and learnings, so that you're actively involved in your learning and your somatic process. I can't recall where I heard this for the first time, but it's so true, *ink makes you think*!

Coming back to your reason for picking up this book, maybe you already have a CSE practice. Or, perhaps, like so many people I've met and worked with, you feel that you've "tried everything" to relieve niggles or movement difficulties but with no long-term relief or change. Are you fed up managing symptoms with pain relief medication and costly treatments? Are you fed up with being in pain and unable to enjoy doing the things you love comfortably, or maybe even at all? If you can relate, I'm delighted for you that you're here! We each have the capacity and ability to make changes in how we function and feel. We also have the ability to continue learning throughout our lives. We don't have to blindly follow the self-fulfilling prophecies that are either given to us by others (in my case, a medical consultant; and who was I to question him?) or those stories and beliefs that we impose upon ourselves. What you're about to embark on may well be a different approach to experiencing yourself than you have previously explored. With this new approach and learning experience comes long-term change from within. The impact of creating change for yourself and regaining control of and connection with yourself is a deeply empowering and profound process. I know this to be true for myself, which I shall share more of later. I also know this to be true for so many of the wonderful people I've had the pleasure of working with and learning from over the years. Those clients have shared comments such as "This has transformed my life," "I can take long walks again," "I can put my socks on," "I sleep well now," "I don't get back pain anymore," and "I feel like I've found myself." The list of such wonderful comments literally goes on and on! I look forward to sharing some client stories with you throughout the following chapters. Where I've shared personal stories, I've taken care to anonymise and change names, to respect my clients' privacy. I'm continually grateful to all of you who have and continue to show up for yourself to classes and clinical sessions, with curiosity, a desire to learn about yourself, and an ever-growing awareness of your process.

Some questions for you to consider

- What would you like to be different about how you move, feel, live?
- What activities do you tell yourself you can't do or can no longer enjoy?
- How much do you believe in your ability to change how you live, move, and feel?

CHAPTER SUMMARY

▸ Long-term change comes from within.

▸ Change starts with awareness.

▸ We each have the capacity and ability to make changes in how we function and feel.

▸ We have the ability to continue learning throughout our lives.

▸ The impact of creating change for yourself and regaining control of and connection with yourself is a deeply empowering and profound process.

▸ This method is rooted in science.

▸ This is so much more than just movement.

CHAPTER 2

What Is Clinical Somatic Education?

This is movement education. It was developed by Thomas Hanna Ph.D. to restore functional movement and to relieve pain and restricted movement caused by unconscious muscle tension. Put simply, it's movement education that teaches us how to relax tight muscles, so we can move and live in our intended functional way with freedom and ease. There are three specific factors that set Hanna's work apart from other somatic approaches and I shall explore each of these in some detail. They are:

Sensory Motor Amnesia
Three stress reflex patterns
Pandiculation

First up is Sensory Motor Amnesia (SMA). Hanna coined this term to describe unconscious chronic muscle tension. Broken down, this literally means we have *forgotten* how to *feel* and *move* our skeletal muscles. Just imagine for a moment how your life would be affected if you could no longer feel or move with control. The most basic of functions, such as breathing, standing upright with ease, or walking freely would take a great deal of effort to perform. Perhaps that surprises you, but, in truth, for so many people, this is indeed the case.

SMA is much like a blind spot in our awareness and it's happening all the time. SMA is learnt and is a habituation. When an action or behaviour is so well learnt it becomes habituated, it becomes like second nature without the need for conscious awareness or effort to perform it. Think of a skill you've learnt, like driving a car. When you started, can you remember how much focus it took to consider every stage of checking: putting your seat belt on, checking the mirrors, turning the ignition, and engaging the transmission? With practise and repetition all of these steps become so well learnt that they feel like "second nature," without conscious step-by-step planning. When an action becomes a habit, the process takes place at the subcortex level of the brain so that we can go about our day with more efficiency and have more "head space" to focus on other things. And thank goodness for our wonderful subcortex, because if we had to consciously consider every aspect of our day, getting out of bed, how to wash, how to dress, it's unlikely we'd ever leave the house!

So whilst learnt behaviour and habituations can help us to get things done, with regard to SMA what is really important to realise is that the more muscle tension we hold, the less efficiently we function. Movement takes more effort and becomes more restricted, energy is used up, everyday activities get harder, and more pressure is put on joints and every part of our system just to exist. I think of SMA as being a bit like a slow puncture in your bike tire. Every day, you keep pushing the pedals to move forward, but it gets harder and harder, and takes more and more effort just to stay balanced and keep moving forward. We might even fall into the trap of telling ourselves things like *Well I'm getting older*, *this is inevitable*, or *it's just part of life*. With these kinds of beliefs, it's no wonder so many of us become victims of our self-fulfilling prophecies. One day, we find that we no longer do the things we used to, and we may end up ditching the bike altogether. And the less we move, the more symptoms of pain or discomfort begin to show up.

Spoiler alert! No matter where we live, what we do, how much money or status we have, we all experience chronic muscle tension / SMA. It is, indeed, the great leveler of class and status. We live our lives without realising we're holding our muscles tight when they don't need to be. And because we don't notice it's happening thanks to it being unconscious, we cannot change it. As Hanna repeatedly talked about, it's impossible to change what we cannot feel. Therefore, awareness is the start of intentionally creating change in how we function and feel. And the really great news about all of this and what underpins this method, is that we always have the ability to continue learning, meaning we always have the ability to create change in how we function.

So what causes us to get really good at holding our muscles tight? A short answer here is to say that life does! Injuries that we experience throughout our lives, physical, emotional, and psychological, cause us to compensate how we move, and for very good reason. If you've ever sprained or broken your ankle or badly stubbed your toe, no doubt you still managed somehow to move around and get to the bathroom. Or perhaps a relationship has ended but you still have to find a way to keep earning money to pay your bills. To avoid more pain and for the injured area, toe or heart, to heal, your nervous system will do a great job of shifting weight from the injured side so that you can hobble around. Or, it will hold you in a deeply protective way so that you can continue to show up each day and do what needs to be done. This all happens unconsciously, and no matter what, you're going to continue getting up and moving forward. In the words of Martin Luther King Jr., *"If you can't fly then run. If you can't run then walk. If you can't walk then crawl. But whatever you do, you have to keep moving forward."* The innate characteristic of a soma is that, no matter what, we will stand up and move forward. And at times, this can only happen through compensatory patterns.

If you've ever had surgery, a traumatic experience for your system despite the accomplishments of modern-day medicine, your muscles will contract and respond to the physical trauma that takes place under the careful hand of the surgeon. If we never consciously release these muscles following surgery and injury, the contractions become habituated and will stay switched on. Then we have the activities that we repeatedly do, such as long hours spent sitting hunched over screens, playing a musical instrument or sport, or doing dozens of sit-ups a day in an attempt to gain a "strong core." When we get really good at doing these activities, we can do them without thinking consciously about every aspect of how to sit, hold a racket, or pick up and play your guitar; it's learnt and, therefore, becomes habituated. Without these things becoming learnt, it's unlikely that we'd ever develop our skills.

So, we have injury, surgery, and activities that we repeatedly do, all of which can contribute to SMA. In addition, we have the context in which we live and how we show up and respond to ourselves and our environment. The layered accumulation of our experiences and how we live our life manifests in how we function, feel, and interact with ourselves and others. Hanna used a beautiful phrase for this, describing our current state as being a *layered presence* of all that has gone before. The accumulation of our life and how it imprints happens on a neurophysiological level. I believe that our experiences and responses to life subconsciously influence our beliefs, decisions, and interactions with our internal and external environment. Therefore, to understand the accumulation of our lived experiences upon how we feel and function, it's necessary to consider the context in which we live: our biological, psychological, and social environments. This method sits within the biopsychosocial model, and from in utero all the way to our last breath, we exist right in the very middle of these parts. I'll talk more on this later in Chapter 8.

Emotions are a physical process and take place within our nervous system and primarily within our muscles. A pretty clear example of this is if you've ever felt nervous before an exam or big decision, you most likely felt sensations and physical changes in your tummy. Therefore, if we repeatedly experience certain emotions, for example fear, worry, or stress as a result of our work, lifestyle, or family environment, we will get really good at holding certain groups of muscles tight. And when we get really good at something, we can do it without thinking.

Chronic muscle tension accumulates over time as we experience more injury, stress, and repeatedly move and hold ourselves in certain ways. It's the *layered presence* mentioned above. Whilst we're unaware of this building tension because it's happening unconsciously, what we do begin to notice, sometimes acutely, are the symptoms. These can show up as pain, asymmetries, health issues, and restricted movement. We tend not to notice the underlying cause, but we definitely notice the symptoms and especially when they speak loudly enough and have us reaching for the pain relief or stop us from doing what we need or love. Have you ever heard someone say, *"I was just picking something up and my back went out!"* Muscle spasms or a sudden pain rarely just happen as we'd like to believe. Rather it's the result of tightness that builds up over time, until there is no more ability for the muscles to move freely. It's a bit like the last straw that broke the camel's back. As we know, it's not that last straw; it's all the loads that went before.

We literally live in a state of ignorance of our ever-decreasing movement and often ignore the warning signs of twinges that come and go. Or even more to our detriment, we accept it as part of getting old, telling ourselves *"It's my age"* and resigning ourselves to it being "normal." Hanna wrote a lot on the subject of aging, which I'll explore further in Chapter 8. These twinges and niggles are all warning signs and messages that we're not at ease. I like to think of symptoms as being like pathways to your unconscious patterns. *If* we choose to follow these paths and listen to these messages, and *if* we create a daily CSE movement practice, we can literally reverse the effects of our unconscious muscle tension and return to moving more freely and functionally; how cool is that?!

Like all habits, what we repeatedly do without question feels normal to us, and by its nature, we tend not to pay attention to our normal. But what SMA does really well is make itself known to us through symptoms. These can show up in many forms such as pain during exercise, restricted movement, and no longer being able to do things we enjoy. Or it may show up in everyday actions like struggling to get up and down from the floor or put socks on without grimacing. One of the many ways that symptoms may show up, and in my experience, this is the number one reason that clients come to me, is muscular pain. There is nothing like pain to motivate us! This can show up anywhere we have skeletal muscles, therefore, everywhere. In my experience, the most common places clients report muscular pain is back, neck, shoulders, hips, knees, and sacroiliac joint discomfort. Then there are the other kinds of symptoms such as low energy levels, poor sleep, shallow breathing, feeling stressed and feeling disconnected or overwhelmed, to name just a few. Listing them all would probably fill another book; I'm sure you get the picture! A typical Western medical approach to such symptoms is to "diagnose, treat, and fix," and what could be more appealing than rocking up to someone's office and being fixed? So much of our culture is aimed towards convenience through services, technology, 24-hour access to shopping and doing what we want when we want. Perhaps "being fixed" is just another aspect of our search for a convenient life. However, that immediate gratification is short lived when we apply it to chronic muscle tension. The author and physician Gabor Maté in *When the Body Says No*, really articulates this dilemma when he writes "*Prescriptions come from the outside, transformation occurs within.*"

Such "fixing" may include medication or visiting medical experts / body work therapists who will attempt to diagnose, treat, fix, and realign us. And herein lies the issue when our symptoms are a result of SMA. When we treat the symptom, relief is likely to be short term because the underlying cause, chronic muscle tension, is still doing its thing from the level of your nervous system. It's a constant internal process that can only be changed for the long term, by you, from the inside.

My client Julie, like many others and myself included, experienced this. After years of regularly visiting chiropractors and massage therapists every time her back spasmed, she came to realise that this was always going to be a temporary solution for what she was experiencing. After just a few months of starting weekly CSE classes, her back spasms had ceased, and she was no longer visiting her chiropractor to be fixed or put right. She had learnt to regain control of her muscles herself, meaning she can use them effectively and most importantly, allow them to relax and lengthen. And because she does this herself, directly addressing the underlying cause of her spasms, she is creating this change for the long term. And an extra bonus, if she now chooses to have a relaxing massage, this will likely be a more enjoyable experience given how much holding tension she has already released herself.

This brings us back to the process of becoming more internally aware and, therefore, somatic in creating our own freedom and long-term change. Coming back to Gabor Maté, he states, *"Prescriptions assume that something needs to be fixed; transformation brings forth the healing – the coming to integrity, to wholeness – of what is already there. While advice and prescriptions may be useful, even more valuable to us is insight into ourselves and the workings of our minds and bodies. Insight, when inspired by the quest for truth, can promote transformation."* Western medicine has accomplished and provides so much, and it isn't my intention to dismiss or argue against this, far from it. It's my view that to empower people to be free and well, we must move beyond our focus of what medicine gives us within a diagnose and fix model. Let's ask what does it not provide, what does it not understand? Top of that list for me would be SMA, including everything that creates it and everything that reduces it.

CHAPTER SUMMARY

► This method was developed by the late Thomas Hanna Ph.D.

► Three distinct factors set this work apart:

  ▷ Sensory motor amnesia (SMA) / chronic muscle tension

  ▷ Three predictable stress reflex patterns

  ▷ Pandiculation

► The impact of our life accumulates and manifests within our nervous system.

► We all experience SMA.

► SMA is learnt.

► SMA is a subconscious process.

► We can reverse the effects of SMA.

CHAPTER 3

The 3 stress reflexes

Hanna identified three predictable full-body reflex patterns that show up in all of us. These reflex patterns are developmental, deep, protective and take place as reflexes do, without any conscious effort or decision making. These reflex patterns are part of what it's to be human, and they enable us to survive, protect ourselves, and keep moving forward. It's fair to say that we absolutely need them. It's only when they become habituated, and we literally cannot move freely out of them, that difficulties and symptoms occur. As Hanna rightly said, long term imbalance, in this respect being held in a particular pattern, won't be tolerated. When these reflexes are repeatedly triggered, or perhaps a one-off experience of such great impact and intensity occurs, we can end up habituating and, therefore, holding these patterns, unable to freely move out of them.

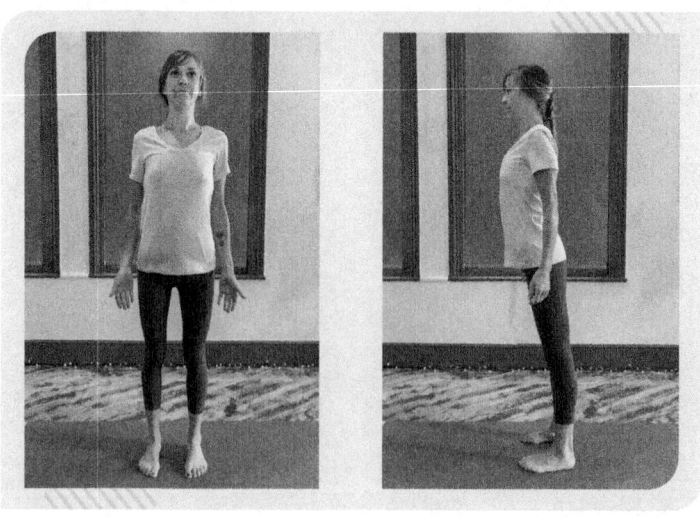

First up is the green light reflex, also known as the Landau reflex. As green light indicates at traffic lights, this reflex pattern is about moving forward and taking action. We begin to experience it at around 3 months old when, laid on our belly, we lift our head to explore our surroundings or find our carer. The muscles along the back of our neck and through our entire back line begin to contract, allowing our head and legs to lift. If you've spent time around babies of this age, notice how they seem to balance effortlessly on their soft round belly with their head and legs hovering in the air. Fast forward several years and decades, and our green light reflex kicks in whenever we're called to action; we've slept through our alarm and suddenly have to jump up out of bed, we're running late for a meeting and need to get there sharpish, we've got a never ending to do list with deadlines to meet or maybe we're a Soldier and need to stand to attention and appear capable, in control, and confident.

A habituated green light reflex refers to holding tension through the muscles of our back and can lead to physical symptoms including back pain, bulging / herniated discs, piriformis syndrome, sciatica, tension headaches, poor sleep, difficulty switching off and resting, tight hips and hamstrings. Regarding move-ment, or lack of it, you may notice it's uncomfortable to lay on your back with legs straight, you may be unable to bend forward with ease to pick things up off the floor or tie your shoelaces, and exercises such as sit ups may feel uncom-fortable and cause neck pain.

Opposite to this is the red light reflex, also known as the startle reflex. It involves a tightening of the muscles through your front including chest, biceps, abdom-inals and inner thigh adductor muscles. As the name suggests and using the traffic light concept, this reflex causes us to slow down and stop and is a deeply protective pattern. If you've suddenly heard a loud noise or somebody pulled a prank on you and made you jump, you'll have experienced just how quickly this reflex happens. Your belly tightens, your eyes squint, your head juts forward and your shoulders jump up to your ears.

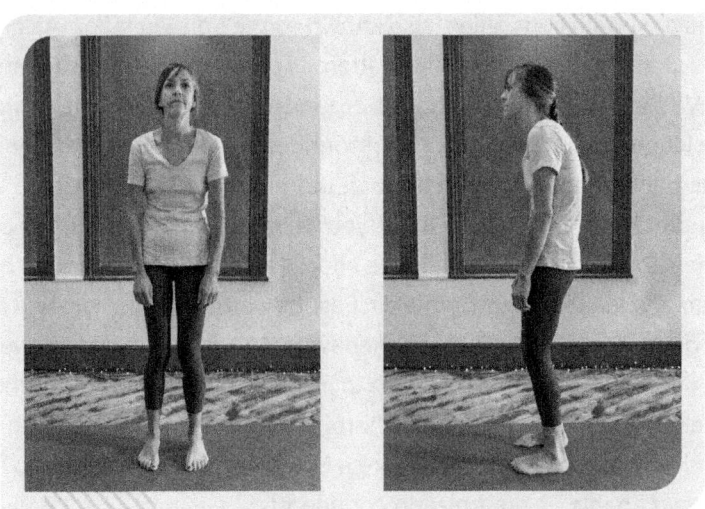

Symptoms caused by a habituated red light reflex include shallow breathing, neck pain, midback pain, tight hips, knee pain and low energy. Movement restrictions as a result of us being stuck in this reflex include difficulty standing or sitting upright with ease, discomfort lying on your front, difficulty lifting up your arms and discomfort during back extension exercises.

The third predictable reflex pattern that Hanna identified is the trauma or "righting" reflex. This refers to an imbalance between our left and right, where one side holds more muscle tension than the other. Whilst the name of this reflex may have a loaded meaning for you, please don't let that put you off. No doubt today's more widespread use of the word trauma is different to what it was in the 1980s and 90s. My understanding is that Hanna used the word "trauma" to relate to physical injury, such as the sprained / broken ankle I mentioned earlier, or one-sided surgery such as appendectomy, or injury such as whiplash. The trauma reflex compensates for such injury and pain, helping us to keep moving forward with some sense of balance. Unlike the name may infer, we may also habituate this reflex pattern through joyful and positive activities and lifestyle. Our individual twists and rotations are one way in which our experiences and repetitive actions manifest, and as such I feel that this reflex pattern can be the most unique in the way that it's an autobiography of our life. Yes, these reflex patterns are predictable, but our individual journey through life, what we experience, when, and how we respond are unique. I appreciate this may sound strange, but because of this, if I *had* to pick a favourite reflex pattern, then the trauma reflex would be mine! So what might those joyful activities be? Well, for starters, think of any sport, dance, or musical instrument. Then there are the additional activities such as being one hand dominant or carrying a shoulder bag always on the same shoulder.

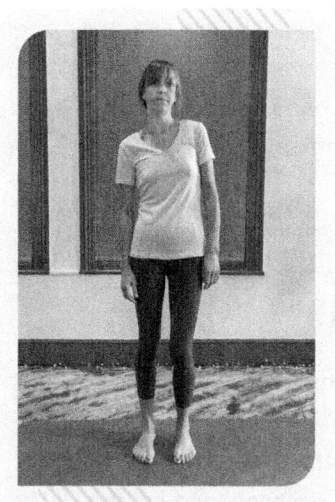

Physical symptoms from a habituated trauma reflex encompasses any one-sided pain; sciatica, hip / knee / neck / shoulder pain, sacroiliac (SI) joint issues. As for how it affects our movement and alignment, you may notice asymmetries such as one shoulder sitting lower than the other, a constant head tilt, less movement through one arm / shoulder / leg / hip, rotational patterns and scoliosis, different eye vision between left and right, and believing we have one leg shorter than the other; structurally this is very uncommon, but is commonly believed and accepted to be the case. I have met many clients who adamantly believed they had one leg shorter than the other, because "that's what I was told years ago." These same clients find that after releasing their chronically tight waist muscles, their legs are in fact the same length. I never tire of bearing witness to this "phenomena" and the astonishment on a client's face, quickly followed by a sense of joy, and balance!

In Part Two, you'll learn how to notice which of these reflex patterns may be habituated for you. In truth, we probably all have a little bit of each of them; however, one may dominate more than the others. Reading the kinds of symptoms listed above for each of the reflexes, you may already have begun to identify with a particular reflex pattern. If so, brilliant, because until we know what we're doing, we cannot do something different. Part Two of this book will guide you through movements in a very deliberate and intentional way, so that you can begin to release out of these holding patterns. In doing so, you'll relieve the symptoms and restricted movement caused by them. Learning how to pandiculate is the process by which you can restore functional and comfortable movement. I'm going to explain how this works in the next chapter. In particular, I'm going to explain how pandiculation lengthens our chronically tight muscles and increases their resting length more effectively than stretching.

CHAPTER SUMMARY

► Hanna identified three predictable reflex patterns: green light, red light, trauma.
► We all experience these reflex patterns.
► These reflexes are necessary and helpful.
► We may have habituated a combination of all three reflexes.
► Discomfort and restricted movement occur when the reflexes become stuck / habituated.
► We want to have the freedom to move into and out of these reflex patterns.
► We can learn to release out of these reflex patterns if they have become habituated.

CHAPTER 4

Pandiculation

This may well be a word you've not come across before; I certainly hadn't before learning about this work. Hanna took this term from the veterinary world, and it literally means to yawn. On that note, when was the last time you had a really satisfying yawn? I look forward to a time when I ask that question and the general response will be *"When I woke up," "Just before I left home,"* or *"When I got up off the sofa."* The usual response I hear is *"I can't remember."* Yawning is our way of relieving tension and energizing ourselves. It's necessary and functional. Animals are great reminders of how often it's good to do this. For those of you who spend time around cats and dogs, you'll see them pandiculating all day long, maybe over 40 times a day, after naps, runs or just changing position. What I was both shocked and fascinated to hear from a fellow certified CSE teacher, is that animals in captivity actually pandiculate less than their counterparts in the wild, in their natural habitat, where they're living as intended. This got me thinking about what that means for us and how we live. If we no longer yawn regularly as our nervous system requires in order to relieve stress, are we, too, living in captivity, in an environment that doesn't serve our function?

When we yawn / pandiculate our muscles, there are two muscular actions taking place. One is that a group of muscles are contracting and shortening, and the other, necessary to allow those contractions, is that another group of muscles are lengthening. We are lengthening and contracting at the same time, a functional and efficient process. For example, to easily bend forward and put your socks on, your front shortens but your back has to be able to lengthen. If holding tension in the back muscles means they cannot release and lengthen, this will restrict our ability to roll forward comfortably and, therefore, restrict the way in which we can function easily. When you learn and experience CSE, you learn how to pandiculate and remember how to yawn your muscles so that they can lengthen and relax. You'll find a step-by-step guide on how to do this in Part Two of this book.

When you practice, learn, and develop your own daily CSE habit, you're reminding yourself of how to feel and move as a whole functional and efficient system. This enables you to relieve tension and to continue enjoying the things you love to do whilst feeling good before, during, *and* after. CSE reminds your muscles to relax, via conscious communication between your brain and your muscles. As the control centre of your system, your brain is telling your muscles what to do. Therefore, for your muscles to intentionally relax, this message comes from the brain.

Mark came to me for clinical sessions because of general stiffness, but especially his tight back and hamstrings. He spent his working days mostly sitting, and his movement passion was running marathons, which he'd been enjoying for many years. But niggles and tightness were beginning to interfere with his running, despite a fairly lengthy stretch routine before and after his runs. What Mark didn't realise at the time was that his stretching routine was never going to relieve his SMA, the underlying cause of his niggles and stiffness. Not only that, but it was potentially making him tighter and exacerbating his symptoms, and here's why. When our muscles are unconsciously held tight, let's say 50% is always held tight, when we stretch, we're only able to lengthen the 50% that isn't chronically contracted. So we may feel some lengthening to that half; however, if we push our stretch beyond that consciously controlled 50%, then our stretch reflex comes to the rescue and pulls us back from the brink. In doing so, our muscles may tighten up even more than just 50%, and our stretch routine has done nothing to increase the overall resting length of the whole muscle. As such, we don't feel any more supple over the long term.

If we're to effectively reduce that 50% of chronic muscle tension, we need to bring the whole of the muscle back under our conscious control. This is where pandiculation comes in. Rather than trying to make the muscles do something they can't (i.e., lengthen), we do more of what they can do, which is shorten. We begin by increasing the contraction, which sends new sensory information to our cortex. It's saying, *"Hey, this muscle I've not felt for a while is doing something new!"* From here, we then slowly, with awareness, begin to release back to rest. As you repeat this process, gradually the resting length of your muscles begin to increase, because they're getting new messages from your cortex (conscious brain) to release and lengthen. This is a different message than they have been getting from your subcortex (subconscious brain where habits "live") to contract and shorten. To contract further into tightness may seem counterintuitive to you, especially where there have been loud messages that we all need to be stretching to be more flexible. Stretching is only going to be effective where we have no resting tension. Despite the complexities of our incredible nervous system, I love that there is a beautiful simplicity to this process. And for those of you who like to get geeky about the science behind this, I'm going to explore this further in the next chapter.

 Some questions for you

- When did you last have a really good spontaneous yawn?
- How often do you yawn throughout your day?
- How often do you stretch?
- How supple does this make you feel in the long term?

CHAPTER SUMMARY

- ▸ Pandiculating is like yawning your muscles long.
- ▸ Pandiculating is how we reverse the effects of chronic muscle tension.
- ▸ It all starts with awareness.
- ▸ Stretching doesn't release chronic muscle tension.

CHAPTER 5

The science bit

Having some understanding of the neurophysiology involved in the process of CSE can aid our understanding of why and how it enables freedom of movement. The science offers a compelling explanation for how and, therefore, why this is an empowering method. The science behind what we as certified CSE teachers do and why we do it's what sets this work apart from the other methods that promise release from muscular pain and associated issues. For those who are yet to experience the feeling of moving somatically or who remain cynical of a method relatively unknown to the general population (at the time of writing that is), the neurophysiological facts provide scientific explanations of how this method can relieve pain and restore functional movement, not as a quick fix, but for long-term freedom. To begin exploring this, it's helpful to have some knowledge about our nervous system; so, let's take a look.

According to Louise Tucker in *An Introduction Guide to Anatomy and Physiology*, the purpose of our brilliant nervous system is to send information and instructions from the brain to the entire system. In return, motor sensory messages are sent from every part of the system back to the brain on a continual feedback loop. This information is sent via neurons in the form of electrical impulses. This process works as a complete communication system, the purpose being to maintain a stable physiological state. To better understand our nervous system, we can initially look at it in two parts: the central nervous system (CNS) and the peripheral nervous system (PNS). Doidge, in *The Brain that Changes Itself*, describes the CNS, which consists of the brain and the spinal cord, as being the *"control and command centre of the system,"* which is apt, given its central location in our body. The PNS connects the CNS with the rest of the body, by sending impulses from the sense receptors to the spinal cord and brain and back to the muscles and glands.

The PNS is further subdivided into the somatic nervous system (SNS) and the autonomic nervous system (ANS). The SNS connects the CNS to our skeletal muscle fibres, giving us voluntary control of our muscles so that we can consciously contract and release them and move our skeleton. We lose this voluntary control through chronic muscle tension, and we learn to restore it through CSE movements. The SNS is the "voluntary" branch of our PNS. It also keeps us safe by responding to stimulus and threat by contracting our muscles into certain patterns. In Chapter 9, I'll speak more about how experiences, emotions, and wounds manifest in our nervous system and, therefore, how this work contributes towards healing.

The ANS, on the other hand, is the involuntary branch of our PNS and serves our smooth muscle functions, such as those located in our gut, eyes, heart, etc. The ANS is further divided into the sympathetic and parasympathetic nervous systems. Our parasympathetic nervous system enables us to relax, rest, and digest, whilst our sympathetic nervous system relates to states of fight and flight. Therefore, these sections add to our entire system's ability to work in a stable and balanced way. These processes take place without our conscious awareness. Our ability to function consciously and subconsciously is therefore dependent upon our nervous system, and we need to be able to do both.

Our nervous system contains different kinds of neurons, varying in structure, location, and the types of impulses that they send. I'm not going to go into detail about all this here; however, of particular relevance to CSE are our sensory and motor neurons. Sensory neurons transmit information about what is happening internally but also externally in our environment. This sensory information is picked up by any of our senses such as touch, smell, or sight. Sensory neurons constantly transmit this information to our brain, which then sends signals to our muscles via the motor neurons, a process Blandine Calais-Germain calls "proprioceptive sense." Motor neurons connect the spinal cord with our muscles and can be further divided into two types: lower motor neurons, which send impulses from the spinal cord out to the muscles, and upper motor neurons, which send impulses between the brain and the spinal cord.

Hanna described our sensory and motor functions as being like two sides of the same coin. They're divided into two parts of the spinal cord but become integrated in the brain. *"The brain integrates the incoming sensory information with outgoing commands to the motor system."* He also described this interplay between our sensory and motor systems as being like a constant loop, full of sensory and motor information.

We can view our nervous system as containing two "maps." These maps can show us where from and where to our nerves innervate our skin and muscles. Our skin contains nerve endings whose job is to relay sensation from the skin to the brain; I like to think of our skin as being the external surface of our brain. Nerves that stem from different parts of the spinal cord connect to different areas of our surface. The lower down our spine the nerve root comes from, the lower on our body the area of skin that it innervates. Dermatomes is the name given to this and can be seen clearly on a dermatome map or diagram.

Similarly, myotomes refer to which spinal nerve root innervates which group of muscles. For example, the muscles in our lower legs are innervated by the nerves that come from the spinal nerve root in our lower back. Myotomes help us to understand why, if you have a bulging disc pressing on the nerves coming from this lower part of your spine, you may experience pain or symptoms in your lower leg or foot. An understanding of myotomes explains why we work from the centre to periphery; where we experience pain is often a symptom of a problem in another area. To use sciatica as an example, focusing on the pain in the leg or foot is never going to address the root cause and, therefore, won't relieve the symptoms long term.

CHAPTER SUMMARY

► CSE is rooted in our neurophysiology.

► Our brain is like the control centre of our system.

► Our nervous system constantly relays sensory and motor information between our brain and our muscles.

► The process of chronic muscle tension and habituation takes place at the level of the subcortex.

► Where we feel pain isn't necessarily where the "problem" is.

► Conscious control of our muscles and whole system takes place at the cortex level.

CHAPTER 6

The science of learning

Learning and creating change is possible because, as Doidge explains in *The Brain That Changes Itself*, our brain is *"plastic and adaptable."* If we're to effectively create change in how we feel and function, understanding what prevents or enables that change is essential. Habits are a consequence of learning, and learning is possible because of plasticity. A skill or a behaviour that once took careful action and conscious awareness of every step, like learning to swim, once practiced and integrated becomes an action that seems like "second nature." We can perform the learned skill automatically without needing to pay conscious attention to every aspect of what we're doing (e.g., we can jump in the pool and swim to the other side without having to think through what to do with our arms and legs; we just do it).

To break this down further, I'll focus on two main areas of our brain that are involved in the process of learning and habit formation. The initial part of learning takes place in the cortex; this is the part of your brain that enables you to learn, plan, reason, and consciously perform tasks. When you join a CSE movement class and you're asked to move and pandiculate with awareness, your teacher is literally asking you to get cortical, to consciously think about and feel what you're doing by paying attention to the detail. The cortex is your system's starting point for learning and, therefore, it's where functional change needs to start. It also explains why when we do our practise, we need to avoid distractions, so that we can pay attention in order to learn.

I like to think of our system as being like a management hierarchy. For the shop floor workers, our muscles in this analogy, to change how they work and what they do, they need to be given new orders from the top. Our cortex is the top, like the CEO of a company. Then we have the sub-cortex, which in this analogy is like the middle management. They will start to change what they tell the shop workers to do, once the CEO (your cortex) gives them new orders. This then frees up the CEO (your cortex) to get on with learning other skills and ways to improve the running of the system. It's like a top-down process.

Another important factor in our learning process is that of feeling and noticing something new or different. When we differentiate movement, we're intention-ally moving in a different way so that we can sense something new or long forgotten. It's a way of distracting the brain from its habitual patterns, by intro-ducing new or forgotten patterns and possibilities. When we differentiate, we're involving three specific parts of the brain: the cortex, cerebellum, and the retic-ular activating system (RAS). These three parts enable us to learn, sense, and respond to stimuli. Hanna, in *The Body of Life*, viewed somas as being able to self-adjust, self-correct and self-change, but only *"if that system is given new information with which to interact and if that system is allowed to become sen-sorily aware that there are other options than the ways in which it habitually functions."* When you join a class or have a clinical session, you have an oppor-tunity to experience movement in a different way, and, therefore, you have an opportunity to experience a difference in what you can feel. This is why when we're moving towards creating change, the emphasis is always on sensing and feeling.

Using the idea of a woodland path to demonstrate neural brain maps offers a visual way to understand this. Imagine you're walking through woodland. You take the same path every day, and each day that path becomes clearer. The grass and shrubs are kept at bay and a groove begins to appear where your footprints tread. The path deepens and widens, so each day, it's clearer and easier to find. This is like the neural pathways that enable you to habituate a behaviour; the more you repeat it, the "deeper" the neural grooves and the more you can do that behaviour without needing to pay conscious attention to it. One day, you take a different path through the woods, which could be like having a one-to-one CSE session or joining a group class. The new alterna-tive path is overgrown, it's difficult to find your way through, and you may not even be sure if it's the right way. As it turns out, this path is better than your regular one and you arrive at your destination sooner than expected, despite possibly feeling confused or perhaps even disorientated at first. I think this is akin to learning to walk freely again and integrating your movements after a class. The older path / the way you used to walk, is still very clear, easier to find and use, and may even feel secure or reassuring. However, this new path has something special to offer and the more you use it, the clearer and easier it becomes. This is akin to differentiation, distracting the brain from its habitual patterns and introducing new or alternative movement patterns and possibilities. Differentiating, doing the same thing but in a different way, involves the cortex, cerebellum, and RAS, three parts of the brain that enable us to learn, sense, and refine movement and coordination.

When you join a CSE class, before exploring a movement, you may be asked to imagine doing it first; this process is called motor planning. You may have heard about athletes doing this, imagining themselves scoring a goal or hitting a winning shot, and for very good reason. When you motor plan a movement, your brain is involved as if you were actually doing the movement. The neurologist Roger Sperry stated that the impact of just thinking about moving affects the motor cortex. Hanna, in *The Body of Life*, highlighted the significance of this in terms of clinical somatic education. *"The implication is that thinking is a physical act. More specifically, it means that thinking is a motor rich act, triggering the motor neurons in the motor cortex, which directly connect with the muscles of the body."* Hanna's belief was further reinforced through research around specific brain cells named mirror neurons. Gregory Hickok, in *The Myth of Mirror Neurons*, states that mirror neurons play a role in enabling us to imitate behaviour, and that, in doing so, there is a neurological response in the brain that converts an observed action to a series of muscle commands. This is why we may have the same mannerisms and movement style as our carers, not because they're inherited, but because they have been learnt through observing and experiencing. This is essential to our survival, as it helps us to form attachment and connection. And if these patterns are learnt, then we know we have the ability to learn new ways of acting and moving. Therefore, we have possibilities to create change in how we function.

When we think about effective learning, this is achieved when we're able to focus on one thing at a time and avoid distractions that take us away from our ability to focus. This is thanks to the parts of our brain that formed early in our development, specifically the amygdala and the RAS. These areas of our brain are like a lighthouse that is always switched on, shining its beam out to sea. This continual "scanning" is ready to alert us to potential distraction, danger or any stimulus that needs to be filtered and processed. Consider just for a moment, how much stimulus you're exposed to every day, perhaps every moment of every day. In fact, can you think of any times when you're exposed to nothing, and nothing is being detected or needing to be filtered through your lighthouse beam? Does considering this help you to appreciate just how "busy" your system is, even when you believe you're not doing anything? This "radar" process means that we can easily become distracted from what we're trying to focus on. This is especially true if we've lived experiences through which we have needed to be alert or vigilant.

According to Rothchild in *The Body Remembers*, to learn effectively, our pre-frontal cortex, the learning and reasoning part, needs to be in balance with our limbic system, the arousal system including the amygdala and RAS. When we have too much stimulus, we can feel distracted or overwhelmed as detailed in *Buddha's Brain* by Hanson & Mendius. For example, how easy is it to concentrate if you're cold, hungry, or there is a lot of noise? Maintaining a sense of balance between these parts of our brain enables us to learn most effectively. You're going to read more about how to apply the science of learning in Part Two. That's where I'm going to take you through a step-by-step guide of how to most effectively do your CSE movement practise.

CHAPTER SUMMARY

- ► Learning and changing how we feel and function is always possible thanks to neuroplasticity.
- ► Chronic muscle tension is learnt.
- ► Learning takes place at the cortex level of the brain.
- ► Our amygdala and RAS are constantly on the lookout for stimuli and can, therefore, reduce our ability to learn effectively.
- ► We learn best when we reduce external distractions.

CHAPTER 7

The science of habits

What is a habit? According to Hanna, they're *"nothing more than the human version of fixed motor patterns."* Put simply, if it's a habit, then it has been learnt.

When a behaviour becomes integrated, the learning and messages to repeat that behaviour or action comes from the subcortex part of our brain. Our subcortex is involved with our involuntary and subconscious actions. If it's become like second nature and we don't have to consciously think about how to perform it, then it's coming from the subcortex. This part of the brain has a faster processing time than the cortex, which enables us to get things done, "do more," and live without being overwhelmed. The subcortex is like the control centre of our reflexes, including our red light, green light, and trauma reflexes. And, significant to understanding chronic muscle tension, it's where our sensory motor amnesia (SMA) "lives." So, whilst the faster processing time can be helpful by enabling us to get lots done, it can also contribute to us becoming less flexible in the way that we function, think, and, therefore, live. I find what Doidge has to say on this matter in *The Brain That Changes Itself* really helpful, terming this phenomenon the "plastic paradox." He describes the "double edged sword" of neuroplasticity as, on one hand, enabling us to continue learning throughout our lives, but, on the other hand, it enables the formation of "stubborn habits."

Whilst habits enable us to refine actions and get really good at a skill, they may also prevent other changes from occurring and affect how we live without us realising the impact that they have. I enjoy how succinctly the author of *Atomic Habits* and keynote speaker James Clear puts it: *"The habits you follow without thinking, often determine the choices you make when you are thinking."*

You may be wondering what this has to do with your symptoms such as tension headaches or hip pain. When muscle contracted becomes habituated, we don't notice the underlying habit, but we do notice the symptoms of pain and / or restricted movement. We notice when we decide not to take that long walk with friends, or a grandparent decides not to play on the floor with their grandchild because they worry that they'll never get back up. As Clear says, *"We are limited by where our habits lead us."* His words accurately describe SMA and the impact that it can have upon how we live.

Despite our individualities, we're all designed the same, with the same control centre and nervous system design. Therefore, we all experience SMA. Understanding how and why behaviours become unconscious and why we lose the ability to feel or control parts of our system underpins CSE. This is why to restore function is an educational experience. We are learning and remembering how to relax, how to restore functional movement, and, my favourite and most profound reason, how to be free and autonomous. Adopting a curious and scientific approach to our practise leads to questions about what we know and don't know. As Adam Grant points out in his book *Think Again*, *"The purpose of learning isn't to reaffirm our beliefs; it's to evolve our beliefs...as we question our current understanding, we become curious about what information we're missing. That search leads us to new discoveries."* Understanding how we function as a whole system and, therefore, how to effectively approach change on a nervous system level, is what underpins CSE.

CHAPTER SUMMARY

- ► Habits are learnt processes and take place subconsciously.
- ► SMA is habituated muscle tension.
- ► We learn new habits by consciously, intentionally, and with awareness repeating an action.
- ► Habits affect how we live.
- ► Habits affect our conscious actions and decisions.

CHAPTER 8

Lifestyle, culture, and stress

I dedicate a chapter to culture and lifestyle in this book for very good reason; CSE sits within the biopsychosocial model. This model helps us to understand how our lives are affected by these three environments: biological, psychological, and societal. CSE is about experiencing and understanding ourselves as a whole system. Through this system, we consider how all aspects of our lives function together and make up our whole existence. To do that and to begin understanding the causes of our discomfort or restricted movement, we must look to the context in which we live. Exploring and beginning to question how society affects and influences how we live and function and what we deem to be important is necessary in moving towards understanding the essence of who we are and what empowers or restricts this.

As I was planning this chapter, there was always one client who kept coming back into my thoughts. As she explored her CSE practise, this client with whom I had the pleasure of working, shared with me that much of her life had been spent trying to be small, to not be seen, and not draw attention to herself, especially whilst out in public. She literally described herself as having built an internal prison from which she existed, and for good reason. She had been born and lived in Iran for the early part of her life and, therefore, had grown up in a culture and society where women's rights to freedom and autonomy are denied and the death penalty is ever present. She described how remaining "small" and not bringing attention to herself was essential for her safety. Unsurprisingly, she had a habituated red light reflex; a deeply protective reflex pattern that puts on our brakes, makes us small, and is how feelings and states of being trapped, fearful, and anxious manifest. As she explored her practise and process, she described a feeling of freeing herself from the constraints of her internal prison, where she'd lived for so long.

Our culture and environment impact our development and how we function, on both conscious and unconscious levels. The differences between these levels are important distinctions to make if we're to better understand ourselves and move towards a life of free will and autonomy. By the nature of unconsciousness, we don't see it, we don't recognise it, and, significantly, we don't question it. It's what we deem to be "normal," expected and "second nature." The very definition of second nature tells us that it isn't our first, but that it's something we've adopted and learnt. Those who know me are well aware of my love of questions, and especially so in my desire to continue moving in the direction of freedom and autonomy. I can't help but ask about the impact that our Western culture and systems of education, public services, politics, and economy have upon our autonomy and free will. What unconscious habits, decisions, and lifestyles does this culture create, that we don't question because we perceive it all as being "normal." Let's not make the mistake of believing that because something is normal, popular, or commonplace, it's healthy, beneficial, or to be tolerated. After all, issues such as back pain and anxiety are common issues for a huge percentage of the population, and I've yet to meet anyone who actually enjoys or wants either of these.

With regard to public services, the culture of our healthcare has a great deal of influence upon how we live. The advances and abilities of Western medical achievements are incredible, and it certainly isn't my intention to dismiss this. To continue towards widespread health and wellbeing, however, it's important to consider and ask in what ways our health services are restricted in enabling us to live well. What lies beyond the confines of Western medicine, and what can be offered to meet the functional needs of any society? Hanna described us as being "self-sensing and self-correcting" organisms. If we never come to realise that we have the ability to sense and correct ourselves, we may continue to reinforce the mutually dependant relationship between patient and "expert" that makes up the Western approach to healthcare. Furthermore, if we don't connect the dots between our lifestyle, being disconnected, stress, and disease, we remain powerless to change our habituated patterns that may be creating and contributing to our discomfort and disconnect. Without becoming aware of and understanding the link between our out-look, in-look, and how we "truly" (not just what we tell ourselves) live, it's hardly surprising that we will continue to seek out methods that can fix us. This is so often the case when it comes to muscular pain. What other option is there? Continued disconnect and power-lessness adds momentum to the approach of "diagnose and fix." Interestingly, according to the *Oxford English Dictionary*, the word "doctor" comes from the Latin *docere*, meaning to guide, to teach, suggesting the roots of this role is to provide an exploratory and educational approach to healthcare. Considering this meaning, CSE offers a way of connecting with ourselves. From a place of connection, we can make more informed and, therefore, more effective choices for our wellbeing, but it starts with us. A woman with whom I worked after just one session told me, *"I feel like I'm starting to have a conversation with myself."* Our nervous system is ready to share, we just need to open the door to having a conversation and listen sensitively and compassionately to such messages. In my experience, being fixed by others doesn't always open that door, but learn-ing how to connect with our own process does.

The divide and debate between the mind and the body dates back centuries. Hanna explored this debate in his lectures and in his book *Bodies in Revolt*. If there is a continued need to pick one over the other, Hanna rightly points out that *"There is never a resolution to this question of the mind / body split."* In my view, it isn't an argument of mind over body or body over mind. Our body doesn't exist without the mind, and, the mind's primary function is movement, which takes place through the physical body. To maintain functional living and be present and connected, consider how beneficial it would be to approach our well-being as a whole, mind and body knitted together in a fully functioning system. Take a car as an analogy. It has all of its functioning parts; the engine has its role to pump the fuel, but it needs the wheels to turn in order to move forward and send you on your journey. The wheels won't turn if the engine isn't running. These parts, and all the processes in between are equally nec-essary for the car to function as a whole unit. If we only view ourselves as a body, we miss the essence of what it is to be us. Simply viewing us and others as bodies, as machines to be used and worked, is a dangerous path and one that robs us of all the joyful things life has to offer. What use is love if we're machines? Without seeing our souls, our process, and the essence of us, all kinds of atrocities have and will continue to take place. As Hanna morbidly pointed out, *genocide is easy when all we see are bodies.* How would each of us, our relationships with ourselves and those around us, our communities and societies differ if we develop and grow with the knowledge that we're these beautiful self-sensing, self-correcting somas. To live with ease and freedom is to be self-aware of our whole system. What if wisdom were viewed as being of the greatest importance and necessity, over that of intellectual knowledge, achievements, or wealth? What kind of world would this look like and how would it feel to live within it?

 Some questions for you to explore.

- What do you feel / notice when you think of yourself as a body?
- What do you feel / notice when you think of yourself as a mind?
- What do you feel / notice when you think of yourself as a soma?

I believe Western culture continues to miss its full potential by reinforcing this centuries-old debate of the mind / body divide. Through this separation of diagnosis and treatment for physical and mental health issues, we're moved further from understanding what it is to be us within the context of our environment. I have no doubt that this leads to ongoing strain upon health services, and a population in pain and suffering asking, *"How did this happen to me?"*

In recent years, there has been an active rise in awareness around mental health. Those in the public eye such as politicians, celebrities, royalty, and athletes all seem to have something to say about it. Don't get me wrong; I believe this is entirely necessary so that this area of our health and lives can be talked about openly and free from stigma, as has not historically been the case. However, if the focus remains upon *"let's talk about it,"* focusing on the symptoms and consequences so that people can get treatment, I fear it may reinforce the cycle of "diagnose and fix," after the harm has been caused. If we learn from a more somatic and holistic approach, to address and make changes at the level of the underlying causes, how would focusing our learning and growth at this level affect our ability to live well? How would focusing upon the underlying level of how we develop and live, help us to self-regulate, to connect with oneself so that we're better able to live with wellness and balance? How could we each create a culture within which this could be normal? Of course, this would require a willingness to take responsibility for ourselves. In particular, we'd be required to challenge the belief that so many of us have, that we're dependent upon others to "fix us," or that our health is someone else's responsibility to diagnose and put right. To achieve this may indeed require a significant cultural change. Having witnessed and experienced time and time again the impact of this work, I believe a CSE approach to understanding and experiencing ourselves can help to move us towards such changes. Until we each live as unified, self-sensing, self-correcting, and autonomous beings, and view others the same, we will continue to misunderstand our lives to some extent. This will continue to be a challenge in a society where greater impor- tance is given to qualifications, academic achievement, and status than wis- dom. Although written in 1980, the somatic pioneer Corola Speads's observa- tions, as cited in Don Hanlon Johnson's book *Bone, Breath & Gesture*, remain just as relevant decades on. *"Unfortunately, intellectual development, not the development of our body sense, is emphasised in our culture. The body sense is applied in reference to pain....as if we should be aware only of discomfort! Thus, many people are deprived of enjoying their own well-being. And they do not become aware early enough when something does begin to go wrong, and thus miss an opportunity to prevent serious trouble."*

 Some questions for you

- When did you last change your mind or question something that you view as "normal"?
- What in your life gives you a feeling of space and / or freedom?
- What do you repeatedly do (activity / hobby / way of coping) that may contribute to your holding patterns, restrictions, and level of ease / discomfort?

Justice and community healing

What if we were to have a somatic informed approach to public services, including healthcare, education, and justice? For example, imagine an educa- tion system through which young people leave with an ability to self-regulate, connect with themselves and others, and be interdependent? What if they left formal education with as much if not more curiosity than when they entered it? Imagine healthcare support that empowers each of us to better understand the link between our illness and how we live our lives and stress that we have experienced. And what if we had a justice system in which people were not shamed or judged but treated by society with compassion and support? This is an area close to my heart, though, I appreciate, not to others. In my view and experience, this approach is far more effective in supporting people to better understand how they have been wounded by their life experiences and, consequently, how they live and function. Is it not a useful measure of a society to recognise how it treats the most vulnerable and those most in need of understanding and kindness if change is to be achieved? Having worked in the role of a probation officer for 18 years, I believe that people on the receiving end of our criminal justice system are often those who express, in one form or another, the most pain, hurt, and vulnerability. In my experience, placing a "war" and, therefore, more tension and conflict on factors such as crime does little to deter it being committed. If that were the case, previous government initiatives promising to be *tough on crime and the causes of crime,* and the threat of prison would have nipped crime in the bud long ago. If focus remains upon being "tough" on the symptoms (i.e., the person, offences, or harm that has been committed), then crime and such harm will continue to be a significant problem within any society. The language we use to describe crime and those who commit crime heavily influences our approach. Terms such as "hardened criminals" or "bad / evil people" don't so much invite an approach of compassion and understanding as they create an *us vs. them* dynamic. *Us vs. them* creates more tension and misunderstanding, justifies a *tough* response, requiring *them* to further defend, armor, and *harden* themselves. We only need to harden and armor ourselves when we feel wounded, hurt, and scared and our needs aren't being met. Such hardening and stress take place on a nervous system level, manifesting as chronic muscle tension. What would it take for someone to be softer instead of harder? What kinds of approaches and society would enable this to become a possibility?

To understand and intervene early in the factors that contribute to a social problem such as crime, is to speak to the underlying causes. Through addressing the underlying cause of any difficulty, long term change can occur. For society to move towards this, awareness and understanding of who we fundamentally are and the type of lifestyle that enables our function and essence to thrive is essential. I don't believe this can be achieved without awareness, compassion, and curiosity. In my view, such changes aren't possible in isolation or by shifting responsibility to someone else or some other government department to fix. Whilst I believe changes take place on an individual basis first, they become incredibly powerful when approached as whole community systems, sending the ripples of such change far and wide.

If I chose one condition by which I want to live my life, then it's freedom. I believe that everyone has the ability to create change for themselves, no matter how big or small. This belief underpinned my decision to work in our Criminal Justice System and become a probation officer. During those years, I worked in roles that focused upon enabling change and supporting people to explore possibilities around freedom and how they could live with more ease. It's humbling, deep, and necessary work. Of the many things I came to appreciate through this work is how choice is such a key principle in considering change of any kind. Hanna pointed out *"We're responsible and capable of healing ourselves.... All human beings are destined to have this, **if we chose.**"* However, to refer back to James Clear, our daily choices and, therefore, our ability to make choices, are constantly being influenced by our unconscious habits. I could easily fill another book to discuss the somatic responses I witnessed of people in court and prison settings, and those who were in and had experienced abusive and controlling lives. Looking at them softly from a CSE understanding, I came to see and better understand how the trauma so many of those with whom I had met and worked was showing up in their very appearance, their holding patterns, their habits *and* responses to life. I was increasingly understanding how their experiences were unconsciously sewn through their nervous systems. As my understanding grew, so did my frustrations around our approach to rehabilitation and our society's and government's approach to making someone "fit." Training and resources have fallen short of helping us to really understand the manifestations of trauma and what would meaningfully help those people who are so deeply stuck in their habituated patterns. I believe that people with whom I worked (on both sides of the justice system!) are desperately in need of a CSE approach: both the movement *and* the philosophy that underpins it. Looking back through this career, whilst my intentions meant well, I cringe at my ignorance that led to my earlier approaches of working with people in my effort to be an obedient and "good" employee. I believe deeply that had I known then what I know now, had CSE knowledge and wisdom been part of my training from the start, I would have been a far more effective probation offi-cer. I would have worked so much more effectively with all those individuals in helping them to be more empowered. I'm not entirely convinced that I have per-manently closed the door to being involved with this world. This is never more obvious to me than when I come across the likes of the Compassionate Prison Project (www.compassionprisonproject.org). The incredibly empowering work that is beginning to be done with those who need it so desperately in order to move towards change and wellness is inspiring and deeply moving. I believe a CSE / somatic-informed approach to working with and supporting people in this area of society has the potential to create powerful change.

Stress

Stress is a word that's used a lot. Common definitions include *pressure or worry caused by problems in somebody's life or by having too much to do.* Symptoms such as anxiety, emotional problems, long-term sickness, and the release of the stress hormone cortisol are also listed as ways in which stress manifests. Definitions are important because how we define, view and understand prob-lems such as these, affect how we approach and work towards changing them. If the definitions we use, our beliefs, and our understanding are missing fun-damental and accurate detail, it makes sense that we're likely to be minimally effective at addressing and alleviating the impact of stress.

When stress becomes habituated and or chronic, the balance of our entire sys-tem is disrupted. Hanna put it succinctly when he said, *"Long term imbalance will not be tolerated."* It won't be long before symptoms show up in the form of aches, pains, functional and movement issues, and disease. Stress literally creates dis-ease as it manifests as inflammation *and* muscle tension. When this tension stays on and is habituated, we lose full function and voluntary con-trol of those muscles where stress manifests. In his book *When the Body Says No*, Gabor Maté references research on stress that identifies loss of control as being one of its 3 contributing factors. The other two factors are uncertainty and lack of information. He could be talking about SMA. SMA results in a lack of internal control and a lack of internal sensory information. It's fair to say that when we have chronic muscle tension, we're limited in our ability to meet our physical and emotional needs. From a sensory motor perspective, we cannot meet needs that we don't know we have. Imagine how being blind to our needs could create feelings of uncertainty; one of the three contributing factors that Maté highlights.

A lack of internal control, proprioception, *and* unsatisfied emotional needs can all trigger a part of the brain known as the HPA axis. This axis sets in motion our stress response, including the limbic system (emotions), the hypothalamus (cortisol), and our sympathetic nervous system (cardiovascular, adrenalin, fight/flight/freeze responses). In his book *The Push*, professional climber Tommy Caldwell articulates how each aspect of this model can contribute to us living within a chronic stressful state: *"Psychological factors such as uncertainty, conflict, lack of control and lack of information are considered the most stressful stimuli and strongly activate the HPA axis."*

Having our needs met can have a calming effect upon our nervous system and turn down our stress response. Meeting our needs may include accessing information such as internal sensations, as well as increasing control, such as being able to voluntarily contract and relax our muscles. CSE is so effective at reducing stress because it enables us to regain control through increasing our sensory awareness. It's deliberate and intentional.

When I think of stress and its link to pain, a particular client springs to mind. Andrew, a man in his late 30s, came to me after suffering years of back pain. He went through the normal healthcare route of assessments and scans, though no medical explanation was given for his constant back pain. As such, he was advised to manage his pain through medication and was sent on his way. On the topic of scans, chronic muscle tension won't show up, but the consequences of it will, such as joint degeneration and skeletal misalignment. Andrew had been in the Army and still carried an identifiable soldier's stance; bolt upright, standing to attention and ready for action; a perfect description of the green light reflex. When we met, he told me that his current lifestyle includes working long hours and is packed full with barely any space for rest, quiet, or just time to be. At the end of one class that Andrew had joined, he was talking about how busy he was and named several pretty significant things he was juggling and needed to complete. During this conversation I mentioned that stress is muscle tension, and muscle tension in our back muscles can cause back pain. At which point his eyes almost popped out of his head and he said "What! But I love the stress, I love being busy!" His look of shock soon shifted to a look of confusion. It was about to dawn on him that how he lives his life and his need for the stress and being continually busy could possibly be contributing to the back pain he'd been enduring for years. And more disconcerting than that, would this mean he would have to make changes to how he lives, what he does and how he manages in order to be pain free. Big questions indeed. As the well-known Hippocrates quotation goes, *"If someone wishes for good health, one must first ask oneself if he is ready to do away with the reasons for his illness. Only then is it possible to help him."* This said, how do we even begin to contemplate giving up the causes of our pain and discomfort in life, if we have no awareness of what they are? The starting point can only be through awareness. Our awareness, and, therefore, our ability to move towards freedom and wellness, has the opportunity to grow when it's fed by curiosity and compassion.

This leads me to consider, as a culture, do we even know how to rest? Do we view and justify rest time as a reward? Perhaps you have found yourself justifying a day off from jobs, doing nothing or a holiday as something you have earned the right to, having worked hard enough, having achieved enough. What does it actually mean to rest? The *Oxford English Dictionary* defines "rest" as *a period of relaxing, sleeping or doing nothing after a period of activity.* The definition of relax is *to rest while you are doing something that you enjoy, especially after work or effort.* So this poses the question, what do you do to rest, relax, de-stress? Having read this far (thank you) and what you have covered about how stress manifests as muscle tension, how far do your de-stressing activities go towards actually relieving stress? I believe it's so important that we make space for the activities that we love, that make us smile and make our soul sing, whether it releases muscle tension or not. What I'm asking you to consider here is what you do, and what your beliefs and intentions are around what you do when it comes to releasing and feeling less stress.

Maybe the TV is one of your go-to habits at the end of a long day. If, like me, you enjoy binge watching a series from the sofa, have you ever noticed how you feel afterwards? Do you feel rejuvenated, energized, less discomfort or like you can move more freely? I'll hazard a guess that the answer is probably no. To move towards functioning in an easier way and reducing our resting level of stress requires an intentional, active, and deliberate approach to reducing the stress that we carry. I was recently introduced to a book called *Rest Is Resistance: Free*

Yourself from Grind Culture and Reclaim Your Life, by Tricia Hersey. She shares a powerful message of how Western culture has turned us into machines, taking us away from what it is to be human and what truly enables us to feel whole and connected. She writes *"We as a culture don't have clarity about what rest is and can be...infants, babies know, but...this inner knowing is slowly stolen from us as we replace it with disconnection...From a young age we begin the slow process of disconnecting from bodies' need to rest and are praised when we work ourselves to exhaustion."* Our continual busyness on personal and cultural levels makes me ask, what are we so busy doing? And what conscious or unconscious patterns are driving our constant and exhausting need to be continually busy.

Gavin Francis, author of *The Lost Art of Convalescence,* speaks to our lack of time to rest, particularly in relation to recovery from illness or surgery. He describes a significant turning point during the 20th century with the introduction of antibiotics. With this came a significant shortening of the time that people were treated for what had previously been life threatening and fatal conditions. *"Time in hospital beds began to be seen as inefficient, wasteful and unnecessary. Some clinicians began to suspect that all that was needed was the right prescription."* He goes on to describe how the time given to recover with the life-saving introduction of antibiotics was further and further reduced until it was no longer deemed necessary, hence the title of his book. But what of the wider implications on our well-being when we no longer see the significance of taking time just to be and recover following illness, injury, or times of busyness.

Pain

Pain is worthy of some page space here, and acknowledging how our society and culture views and responds to it. Definitions of pain speak to physical suffering caused by injury or illness and refer to the use of tablets and medication to relieve it. Go to a pharmacy and there are shelves upon shelves full of tablets promising fast pain relief. Switch on the TV and it won't be long before you see an advert for *hard and fast pain relief* that is *tough on pain.* Pain relief in shops is often placed next to plasters and bandages. I find this ironic, because pain relief for addressing symptoms of SMA such as tension headaches and back pain, is akin to sticking a plaster on a gaping wound. Whilst it may ease the symptoms in the short term, enabling us to get something done or have some short-term relief, it's rarely the solution to a recurring problem because it doesn't address the underlying cause. How much does medication help you to understand why you're in pain and what you may need to change or do differently so that it doesn't keep coming back?

Imagine if these shelves were also stacked with information about CSE teachers, even a mirror, to help you remember that you're fundamental in healing yourself, and that only you know how it feels to live as you. No amount of training or experience that professionals achieve can ever enable them to know how it feels to be you. Therefore, doesn't it make sense for you to be at the forefront of your "treatment"?

For some, the word "pain" can have disempowering connotations, almost a helplessness to it. Maybe you can think of someone in chronic muscular pain who feels like they have no control over their life. Maybe they've even resigned themselves to it for the long term. Sometimes, talking about our pain can lead us to feel powerless and put us further into a victim state, from which change becomes more and more difficult to achieve or even believe. Maybe we talk about our pain being the result of something that happened to us, that we were helpless or powerless to deal with. Or perhaps it feeds into and reinforces beliefs that we're unworthy of health and well-being, happiness, and having good things happen to us or that we're not able / allowed to be content. Whatever your story, it's highly likely to be your reality.

 ### Some questions for you

- Say the word "pain" out loud. What do you notice?
- Might it be a part of your identity?
- Is it possible that your pain is linked to a certain place or belief/story?
- What if you could shift or let go of that?
- Does pain keep you in your comfort zone because it's familiar, you think you deserve it, or another reason?
- Do you have a pattern of pain, and does it change?
- Do you believe there's something you can do to reduce your pain?
- Do you believe what you think and feel and how you live your life is related to your pain?

Aging

What does the word "aging" mean to you? What kinds of feelings, thoughts and images does it conjure up? It's hard to escape the negative connotations associated with our aging process. It seems so many areas of culture and society have been infiltrated with endless procedures, miracles, and tactics that are designed to halt, slow down, or even "reverse" it. The extent that people are willing to go to appear younger than their chronological years seem to span far and wide. The effects of such being anything from subtle to the extreme. In some cases, people are willing to significantly affect their function in their pursuit of appearing young, such as reducing their ability to move their faces, express emotion and, therefore, connect with others. What does it say about our culture that this is becoming increasingly normal?

The power of our preconceived ideas around aging and what it means to age, has a deeply significant impact upon us. It affects how we live, how we're expected to be, and what we're expected to have achieved. I'd argue that it goes as far as to impact how we're expected to act at certain ages, thereby determining how we live in order to meet the expectations of our society. To not meet these marks can so often be viewed as a sign of failure, regardless of whether they enable us to thrive. Then combine this with our beliefs that to age is to degrade, degenerate, and deteriorate. No wonder we do all we can to slow it, avoid it, and stop it! Furthermore, if we're continually seeking the unattainable, in this case to be younger than our chronological years, how does that interfere with our ability to be present, as opposed to embracing our years and not being defined by them and the commonly held self-fulfilling prophecies?

Consider time and ageing as being like two sides of the same coin. As mentioned previously, our ability to be present is fundamental to our ability to connect with ourselves and others and to create long-term change. To cease grasping at the unattainable, in this case the unattainable being to be younger, is to begin accepting who we fundamentally are. Is it possible that the more we desire the unattainable, the less connected we are and the less we're in the here and now? Take the idea of grasping at time and needing to slow it down as we age. Have you noticed how as a child, a year seems to be so long, and yet as we age, that same duration of a year seems to pass by so quickly? It's the same length of time; so, what changes? If as we age, we become less connected to the present moment. Then, is it fair to say that we notice, feel, and experience less? Perhaps this leaves very little to mark time, and it becomes a blur that seemingly passes in the blink of an eye, for there is little that we "felt" to mark it. I've noticed for myself that when I'm more present, it's as if time slows down. Perhaps you've noticed this for yourself?

What if aging were an experience to embrace? What if being 80 was utterly awesome and an existence to aspire to? Tom Hanna wrote and spoke much on the topic of the aging aspect of our existence. He even created a whole program of lessons that he called the Myth of Aging. It was reading his book *Somatics: Reawakening the Mind's Control of Movement, Flexibility and Health* that confirmed my long-held beliefs that to gain years of life is something to be embraced and celebrated. My friends no doubt tire of my excitement around birthdays and predictable challenges when I hear their comments of, *ugh I feel old, I don't want to be 40, I wish I were 20 again.* Hanna defines aging as a process in which we become taller and deeper and fuller. The direction our lives take isn't fixed but open. The comparisons he makes between youth and more years I find powerful and moving. He writes, "*Youth is not a state to be preserved but a state to be transcended...Unless we understand that life and aging are a process of growth and progress, we will never know the first principles of living.*"

Rather than taking *a war on death*, what if we embraced aging with softness and inclusiveness and as an aspect of our existence to be relished. As Frank Forencish refers to in his book *Exuberant Animal*, a war on anything creates tension and conflict and disconnect. Alternatively, inclusion creates warmth and softness and understanding. What if we're *"free to change the stories by which we live,"* as the author Daniel Taylor suggests in his book *The Healing Power of Stories*? What if we changed the stories that we hold onto about our aging process? How would that change the way we experience ourselves, how we show up in life and the way by which we live? What if we begin to recognise that we age how we habitually live, and possibly die how we live and age? And, whilst this next suggestion may be a step too far for some of you, what if we embraced and cherished our wrinkles and grey hair, instead of the shame and embarrassment and the need to hide them that many feel? What if we believed that to age, as Hanna said, is to grow deeper, taller, and wiser? What if we lived within a culture that celebrates and embraces wisdom?

CHAPTER SUMMARY

► CSE sits within the biopsychosocial model.

► We cannot separate ourselves from these three environmental factors: biological, psychological, and societal.

► How we live accumulates over time, subconsciously affecting how we feel and function and the decisions that we make about our lives.

► Somatic informed public services can empower whole communities towards freedom and autonomy.

► Stress manifests as muscle tension.

► To reduce chronic stress for the long term requires an intentional and deliberate act.

► To deny and avoid our aging process is to deny a fundamental aspect of who we are.

CHAPTER 9

Movement towards healing and wholeness.

This is so much more than just movement.

A phrase I often find myself using. I couldn't entertain writing this book without taking time and space to explore the profound connection between CSE, the impact of trauma, and moving towards wholeness. To succinctly describe the impact of CSE upon my existence thus far (at times this is easier said than done!), then healing and moving towards wholeness takes centre stage. As mentioned previously, symptoms of chronic muscle tension include a loss of internal feeling, awareness, and control; we become proprioceptively illiterate and increasingly immobile. When this happens, we literally lose our ability to feel and function efficiently as the whole system that we're designed to be. We experience all of life through our nervous system, and through its functions, we're able to feel, see, hear, and respond to our physiological, emotional, and psychological needs. Wherever we have chronic muscle tension, we have obstacles to these messages flowing through our system. Not only does this cause us to become disconnected from and lose control of parts of ourselves but we also become less able to meet our needs that would otherwise keep us functioning well and feeling good. These "obstacles" are a bit like pressing mute on your TV remote control. We may still be able to see a lot of what is happening, but we miss out on the detail and fundamental messages of what's taking place. Unknowingly, our responses and decision making are no longer based upon the full picture.

As somas, we're living, sensing organisms that have the innate ability, as Hanna explained, to be self-correcting and self-determining. To fully understand ourselves and how we function, we need to consider the environment and culture outside of ourselves, which you explored a little of in the previous chapter. We are an entwinned product of the biological, environmental, and societal world in which we're conceived, grow, develop, live, and die. If we're to understand our difficulties and how we can effectively move towards wholeness, being aware and learning to understand the context of our existence within the biopsychosocial model I talked about in Chapter 8, is key. In particular, better understanding how the areas of this model contribute to us becoming separated, disconnected, and immobilised.

Whilst I understand the reasons, separating our physical and mental health creates limitations in our move towards wholeness. In my opinion, Western medicine's general approach to addressing trauma and psychosomatic difficulties is confined by not always viewing us as whole systems within the context in which we live. This "separation" was an ever-present factor through my work in the Criminal Justice System, especially in sentencing practises. Information was sought on an individual's health, and then, separately, came questions about their mental health. This often felt as if it were a token question / inquiry, and as a separate factor in someone's life, rather than the foundation from which someone functions and exists. The neurologist O'Sullivan, author of *It's All in Your Head*, defines psychosomatic illness as a physical illness or condition that is caused or aggravated by mental / psychological stress; it's a combination of mind and body. Are there any illnesses that don't, in some way, affect or are part of both our mind *and* our body? If someone is experiencing physical illness or an imbalance of any kind, how likely is it that they're not experiencing a level of emotional dis-ease? Is it even possible to separate the two? O'Sullivan describes how the term "psychosomatic" is itself not a diagnosis. Therefore, perhaps it's unsurprising that this label causes challenges for Western medicine in which a diagnosis is sought to fulfill its aims of finding a treatment with which to fix the patient. As she points out, *"I have found myself astounded by the degree of disability that can arise as a result of psychosomatic illness."* O'Sullivan relates how, in her experience, patients being treated for psychosomatic illnesses are left with *"no satisfactory understanding of what was wrong."* In my experience, not understanding and lacking insight can lead to feelings of helplessness, and change can seem impossible. Is this not the opposite to feeling empowered and being able to take responsibility and make changes for ourselves as the self-correcting and self-determining somas that we are?

It may be the circles in which I move, but over recent years I have felt and seen the beginnings of a cultural shift in different messages and information seeping into the mainstream around trauma and healing. To name just a few (I appreciate there are *many*), this includes work and research by the likes of Gabor Maté, Irene Lyons, Bessel Van der Kolk and Richard Schwartz. Approaches, research and the many anecdotal stories from their work bring awareness to the felt sense and encourage us to question what we think to be true. Such approaches encourage us to connect with our internal felt sense during the process of intentional healing. In the wider sense of the word, these incorporate a somatic approach to healing, bringing focus back to the felt sense and autonomy back to the individual; they're the expert on themselves. An underpinning theme in what are being described as groundbreaking approaches such as these, is the compassion and lack of judgment with which they're used. In moving towards meaningful and long-lasting change, going to war with your demons or ailments or working harder is counterproductive. Intentions and language such as war and fight can add tension to tension, leading to frustration and increased defenses.

Healing and moving towards wholeness isn't just about knowing, but must also be about feeling different, feeling a change. It's a feeling experience and process. There's a pivotal scene in the film *Good Will Hunting* that highlights this point so sweetly. Sean, the Counsellor played by Robin Williams, sits on a bench with Will, the client played by Matt Damon, after their previously tricky first session. Sean makes the point that Will knows a lot of shit, but he has no experience of how that knowledge *feels*, how it is to actually experience and live the knowledge that he speaks so confidently about. When it comes to healing, gaining knowledge and intellectualising our experiences only gets us so far. The phrase *we cannot think ourselves out of a feeling problem* springs to mind here, along with the neuroscientist Antonio Damasio's view, as cited by Rothschild, that *"just projecting a cognitive judgement is not enough; it's the feel of it that counts."*

To effectively step into our truth, we must move into the realm of feeling, else our understanding and, therefore, our ability to move towards wholeness will always be somewhat limited. Movement is a way to access such changes in feeling. According to Bessel Van der Kolk, in *The Body Keeps the Score,* our brain's primary function is to move, therefore it seems understandable that movement would play a significant role in our healing process. The significance and importance of being able to put words to and articulate sensations and experiences is necessary. However, to only think and talk about problems and difficulties that are embedded within our nervous system doesn't give us the full extent of our ability to heal ourselves. After all, an impact of trauma is to become immobilized; the opposite of this is to move. This has long been known and understood by any therapist who recognises themselves and their clients as whole somatic systems and processes. The importance of listening and responding to our nonverbal communication is nothing new. Sensorimotor and somatic psychotherapeutic approaches aren't new but have been sidetracked and, at worst, ignored and denied as significant within Western approaches to healing. To ignore the nonverbal communication taking place within our body, is to ignore most sensory information that travels between our organs and our brain. Most of these messages travel to the brain, not from it. Hence the importance of including a bottom-up approach to healing and listening to the messages that our nervous system and feeling sense are sharing.

To effectively move towards long-term healing, awareness, kindness, and understanding are fundamental approaches. These enable us to begin considering how each aspect of our being plays a part within our whole system. To understand symptoms and move towards wholeness, it's necessary to look at the whole picture and context within which they're framed. An educational somatic process enables us to move towards wholeness, to live with ease, freedom, and autonomy by helping us to better understand. To move towards wholeness we need agency and to feel empowered. This is gained through a somatic education approach in which we're active participants. This may be a far cry from the approach many of us have experienced as patients passively receiving labels and fixes, the very nature of which can lead to feeling disempowered. I hope that acknowledging and beginning to explore the differences between passive treatment-based approaches and educational somatic methods, more responsive and effective support will open up to us all. And just maybe, those of us who disregard the benefits of and need to move towards wholeness and greater connection, or those who believe themselves to be beyond help, can begin to explore the slightest glimmer of possibilities for change.

The analogy of peeling an onion to reveal the accumulative layers of life's impact and experiences upon us is one with which many of us are familiar. In my experience of both witnessing and feeling the impact of clinical somatic education, the analogy of peeling away layers to reveal truth and connection feels very apt. As layers are peeled away, we begin to feel and become aware of new or long forgotten messages and sensations as they're revealed. When received compassionately and with curiosity, these experiences can open doors towards further awareness and healing. Through CSE, I first became aware of the extent to which my life experiences had manifested, and where subconscious wounding had embedded. Because it was subconscious, I had *no* awareness it was there or how it was restricting me. Rosa Luxemburg sum this up nicely; *"Those who do not move do not notice their chains."* I only began to notice my chains when I was guided through movements that began to release these subconscious holding patterns. Imagine the dent to my pride having believed myself to be someone who "had it sorted," only to find that what I actually had sorted were some very capable and deeply embedded coping mechanisms that I had assumed were the "real me," my authentic personality. Becoming aware of how little control I actually had, compared to what I had believed, and the extent to which I lacked internal awareness, is messy, uncomfortable and, at times, downright scary. I totally get why people would rather not go there and clamp that lid back on! These necessary coping mechanisms help us to survive, but as the armor builds up and accumulates, it interferes with not only knowing ourselves but also others knowing us. As such and understandably, the depth of our connection to ourselves and others will be less. Put that into the context of knowing that our survival is dependent upon connection. Whilst we may not recognise or feel our coping mechanisms and armor because they're our normal, they may eventually show up in symptoms such as physical pain, avoidance, lack of sleep, irritability, being dysregulated, and autoimmune illnesses. When they make their presence known, what if instead of trying to fix our symptoms we asked ourselves *what are my symptoms trying to tell me, what can I learn from them?* Judgment and needing to fix won't lead us down this path, but compassion and curiosity certainly will.

Rothschild, in *The Body Remembers*, wrote about how our somatic nervous system *"encodes traumatic experiences in the brain"* and responds to what we perceive as being harmful through muscle contractions. Therefore, when we intentionally go into our muscular holding patterns, we may be recalling long-held memories stored within our nervous system. Intentionally releasing these holding patterns as we pandiculate, is to physiologically notice and release what we've been unconsciously holding onto, perhaps for years, even decades. For some, experiencing and releasing the depth and intensity of such patterns can be profound and surprising. These experiences enable us to continue getting to know ourselves and moving towards wholeness. But are you ready to meet yourself? Do you even want to? I don't mean the version of you created through and as a result of your environment, experiences, and unconscious patterns. I'm talking about the essence of you and the fundamental aspect of what it is to be a soma. How much effort and energy, consciously and subconsciously, might you have put into avoiding meeting and knowing yourself?

Becoming more regulated and moving towards wellness may require change, and change requires our nervous system to be fed different information. If we want a different output, we need a different input. During a weekend workshop, a member of the group shared how, for many years, she identified as being a stiff and uptight person. This is a message she repeatedly told herself over years, and, as such, she would avoid going to certain places or doing certain and different things. Deeply held beliefs hold a great deal of power and influence over how we feel, function, and relate to ourselves and others. They literally weave through the core of our being. James Clear, in *Atomic Habits*, explains how "identity sustains a habit," and when we think about chronic muscle tension, we're talking about habituation. With that in mind and in relation to your own healing, what stories and identities do you tell yourself that maintain how you live and what opportunities you believe are or aren't possible and available to you? By the end of the weekend course, this same member of the group was reflecting on how she can do far more than she'd been telling herself she was capable of. She came to the realisation that the belief she had been tightly holding onto was no longer serving her well. She came to realise that her potential for creating more freedom, joy, and comfort in her life was far greater than she had imagined. She had found her chains, and she was beginning to loosen their grip upon her.

The challenge with any change, no matter how seemingly unhelpful our current ways may be, is that change and what is unfamiliar to us can be uncomfortable, possibly even frightening. We have no idea where we stand with it or how it will be, to exist differently. I have witnessed this repeatedly through my own experiences, that of my clients, and through my work in the Criminal Justice System. No matter how destructive, harmful, or painful someone's life feels or appears to be, to change that for something that's unknown isn't an easy step or decision to make. As such, we dig in our heels and stick to what we know. So why do so many of us find change to be a scary concept, even if it's towards healing and wholeness? I find what Tibetan Buddhist Lama Sogyal Rinpoche, in *The Tibetan Book of Living and Dying,* had to say on this as being particularly helpful. He writes *"We assume, stubbornly and unquestioningly, that permanence provides security and impermanence does not."* If we indulge in considering the idea and possibility of impermanence, that nothing is fixed, might that enable us to move towards being more present and, therefore, more effective at meeting our needs? Consider this. If we believe aspects of our existence and ailments to be permanent, there would be no need to pay attention to the here and now, for tomorrow will be the same and the day after that and so on. However, if we're to consider that every moment is new, then to avoid the here and now is to avoid being present, grounded, and connected. Our somatic movement practise is an opportunity to connect to the here and now and be present. Whether we're practicing for the first time or we've explored it hundreds of times before, what we've never done is explore it in that present moment. In that moment, there's no telling what may show up for us, what we may feel and, therefore, what we need to explore to learn and create space for ourselves.

When we consider how we can create long-term change for a more comfortable life, understanding how our life experiences have manifested and how we identify with ourselves is key. It can sound simple; it can feel far from it. Perhaps change requires us to step towards our vulnerability? The social science research Professor Brené Brown, in *Daring Greatly*, describes vulnerability as being *"the birthplace of love, belonging, joy, courage, empathy, and creativity."* I can't think of many things that make us feel more vulnerable than stepping away from what's familiar and what we believe about ourselves and others. To step towards an alternative that perhaps we can't even yet imagine or believe even exists, as if it were like some fairytale story, takes courage.

But just what if we open that door and take a peek, maybe even take a step through? Just what if...?

I resonate with people's frustrations in their striving towards "being healed," in what can feel like a never-ending uphill struggle in their attempt to fix themselves. After all, there is an end in sight when we step along the "fix it" path. Just when they feel they've reached the top of the struggle or believe they've found the magic cure to being "healed," they find there's another peak lurking in the distance; ugh! I know only too well how exhausting and overwhelming such thoughts and feelings can be. They're often followed by frustration, stress, and tension; the very symptoms that we're often desperate to relieve. Then I'm reminded of the fact that we're a continual living process, right up unto our last breath. Knowing that, as a soma, we're a living process, entirely changes my relationship and response to the idea that to be "healed" is a goal to get to and set up camp; it's not. Healing and wholeness aren't final destinations, but experiences to move towards. I don't feel it's so much a case of us being a work in progress to be worked upon and "improved"; rather, we're an active process to explore and experience. Shifting from a focus upon fixing, comes space and softness, from which we're more able to create meaningful and long-term change in how we feel and function. Viewing ourselves as a process is also a reminder that we're never the same from one moment to the next. As you read the words on this page, you've never before been in this moment. Life happens every day, and our responses to life, whatever that may be, happen every day. Our experiences from every day, layer and accumulate; therefore, our intention of moving towards wholeness is also a continual process *and* decision. Committing to your own healing and connection isn't a one-time-only agreement. I believe this commitment is a way of living where we check in with ourselves to be present and notice what effect our experiences are having upon us in any given moment. We're giving ourselves an opportunity to feel and see ourselves with fresh eyes, despite having seen and felt ourselves many times before. Adam Grant describes this experience as *vuja de,* as opposed to the experience of repeating the same experience as in déjà vu. Our somatic movement practice is a way of being present to our process at any point that we choose to take a moment to send our awareness to our internal felt sense. From that place of awareness and curiosity, we create possibilities for change. It's the experience of ourselves as being a whole system, a soma, not separate body and mind that enable this; as Thich Nhat Hanh said in *Body and Mind Are One*, "*When your body and mind work together as one, you are fully and naturally present in the moment.*"

The impact of this work on healing and our approaches to this is an area of particular interest for me. Every time I take a step in the direction of my own truth and wholeness, the more I come to consider the similarities between experiences of dissociation and sensory motor amnesia. I understand both to be reflexive and unconscious processes that keep us safe, enable us to survive, and protect us. Both are processes through which trauma manifests at the level of our nervous system. During states of dissociation, fight, flight, our sympathetic nervous system "takes over." When these ways of coping and functioning become habituated and aren't needed in response to what is actually taking place outside of ourselves, then they no longer serve us. When they're habituated, we're showing signs of being traumatized and our possibilities for being present and connected are reduced or are potentially not even an accessible option. To restore balance and return to a state of being present, a state of rest and digest, our parasympathetic system needs to "step forward" and help to rebalance us. Our somatic movement practise is a way of enabling this. It effectively offers an opportunity to restore connection and balance at the level of our nervous system. Creating change at this level is where we change our habits and the unconscious patterns that have been driving us and contributing to our symptoms. Change at the level of our nervous system is how we create change for the long term. This is possible for all of us. Creating more freedom and restoring function is possible when we pay attention, when we're aware and when we're present. As Rothschild states in *The Body Remembers*, "*Awareness of current body sensations can anchor one in the present, here and now...Consciousness of current sensory stimuli is our primary link to the here and now; it's also a direct link to our emotions.*" As such, CSE has a fundamental and essential part to play in the role of addressing and healing from trauma.

As mentioned back in Chapter 1, it's fair to say that I had very effectively disregarded and to a large extent subconsciously avoided the impact of my life prior to my broken back. Fortunately, that was the catalyst that led me to finding CSE, and I have never been more grateful for my lack of equestrian skills! I have come to feel, understand, and appreciate how much I was and continue to be in need of this work in my life. I like to think I would have somehow found it through another path had I been a more competent rider. But we don't know what we don't know, and, for me, until I experienced myself differently and really began to listen to my internal process, I had no idea of what I was in need of in order to exist in a more regulated and connected state. My somatic learning has opened me up to other approaches and support to continue in this direction. Whilst healing can be a messy, confusing, and scary experience, I would choose autonomy and freedom any day, over a continued existence of amnesia, of not knowing and being driven by my unconscious patterns and coping mechanisms. This is totally unlike the character Cypher in *The Matrix*, who just can't resist the "taste" of steak and, therefore, chooses a life of ignorance and being controlled by the "state." What about you?

As the availability and awareness of somatic-informed approaches continue to grow, as do the far-reaching ripples; I believe there's no limit to how far these can flow. CSE reminds us that we're sensory organisms who are made to feel, connect, and move forward. When we feel, we can hear and choose to listen to our needs. When we listen to our needs, we can choose to meet them. From the moment we were born, we didn't hesitate to listen to our needs and do what we needed in order to have them met. What changed? Culture, lifestyle, the manifestation of trauma? You have everything you need to remember how it's to be your free and autonomous self. The next chapter will explain how you can begin this process and learn how to connect, be present, restore function, and move towards wholeness through somatic movement.

CHAPTER SUMMARY

► Our nervous system responds to harm and threat and helps us to survive through patterns of muscle contraction.

► These patterns can be held and stored unconsciously for years, until we intentionally release them.

► Somatic movement combined with talking therapies is an effective and powerful approach to restoring wholeness and healing.

► Somatic approaches to healing are empowering, the opposite of helplessness and dependency.

► Somatic approaches to healing offer us agency, autonomy, and freedom.

► Change may require us to step towards and through a place of vulnerability and discomfort.

► When we practise somatic movements, we're practicing our ability to be present.

► Our symptoms offer learning opportunities if we listen.

► Somatic movement activates our parasympathetic nervous system.

PART 2

The movements

CHAPTER 10

How we do the movements and why

How you do this practise is key to creating long term change in reducing pain and restoring functional movement. I cannot emphasise that enough. It's ALL about the *how*. In this chapter, I'll explain the most effective way to do your practise, so that you can enjoy pain free and comfortable movement throughout your life.

A necessary distinction to make between this and other approaches to movement that you may be familiar with, is that this isn't exercise. No doubt you're aware of and have probably experienced all kinds of exercise such as Pilates, running, team sports, hiking, cross fit, HIIT, or even types of yoga classes; the list goes on and on. Exercise often has a focus or intention upon refining a particular movement, nailing a certain exercise, working hard, burning fat / calories, hitting a goal, beating your personal best, or winning. These goals can give us a great sense of achievement, boost confidence and charge us with those feel-good hits of endorphins. Or, maybe you experience exercise as something to be done because you feel you should do it. Perhaps you find yourself going through the motions of whatever class or routine you're in, counting down the minutes until it's over, and just getting it done.

Our intention of practicing somatic movements is to take time, be present, focus on sensing, and notice what shows up for us in the moment. It's almost as if we're not trying to "achieve" any particular outcome or reach any particular goal. When we let go of a desired outcome and cease any grasping, we can get curious. When we're curious, we open ourselves up to all that may unfold, not just the path that takes us to our goal or intended landing place.

Because this is movement education as opposed to exercise, being curious is the perfect foundation from which to learn and explore. As Ian Leslie puts it, *"Curiosity supercharges learning,"* and *if* we were to have a goal here, it's to learn by increasing awareness and experiencing something different.

Below are my top tips on how to approach your somatic movement practise:

- Soma scans

Soma scans are as important as the movements themselves.

Take time before and after your movements for a soma scan. Taking a scan at the start of your practise gives you a chance to be present, bring your focus internally, and notice where you're starting from. Listening to what you need in that moment will give you information about where you're holding tension, and, therefore, which movements will be most helpful for you. You're responding to what shows up in a moment that you have never been in before. It will also give you a moment to notice any areas that are more difficult to sense and feel. This is important and full of learning because not being able to feel certain areas is one of the ways that chronic muscle tension shows up. Taking a scan after your movements then allows you to feel the effects of what you did and what changes you created. In education, we learn by noticing new and different information and, in particular, experiencing and feeling that new information. Soma scans give us the time we need to notice, acknowledge, and digest that information. You can take a soma scan in any position, be that standing, sitting, or lying down. In fact, we benefit from taking a soma scan not only when we're doing some movements but also at any time, giving yourself a moment to be present and notice how you're moving and holding yourself.

- Where can I do my practise?

As you explore the movements in this book, you'll mostly be doing your practise down on the floor. That's also likely to be the case when you join a class. In this position, we have more of ourselves in contact with the ground. The floor is an invaluable resource for giving us feedback about how we hold ourselves, how we move and how our SMA shows up. Lying down also provides more opportunity for our muscles to relax because we're not working so much against gravity here. So there are good reasons why so much of our practise is done on the floor. However, we also want to explore our practise in different ways. Given that we live much of our lives on our feet and sitting down, I'll also guide you through some seated and standing movements that you can more easily incorporate into your day. This is also really helpful if you don't have the space or environment in which to be able to lie down. You can still explore your practise and release tension no matter where you are.

- Reduce and minimise distractions

You may recall from Chapter 6 The Science of Learning, I talked about how parts of our brain are always on the lookout for stimulus that needs to be filtered and processed. Anything that our "radar (amygdala / RAS) picks up and needs to process does a great job of distracting us from anything else. Therefore, learning is most effectively achieved when we're able to focus on one thing at a time and avoid distractions that take us away from our ability to focus. Those distractions might include the TV or radio, a busy environment with other people around talking or making noise, being too cold or too hot. And my favourite distraction of all, pets; how they love to come for a cuddle or think it's play time as soon as we get down on the floor!

Where possible, set the scene and the environment for your practice where you're able to focus your awareness internally; shut the door, put on an extra layer for warmth and turn off the TV!

Another distraction can be sight. If comfortable to, explore your movements with your eyes closed so that you can focus on your internal sensations rather than what you're seeing outside of yourself. If closing your eyes doesn't feel okay, sometimes this can affect balance or feel overwhelming / unsafe, try keeping your eyes softly open, without trying to fix your gaze or glare intently.

- Move within your range of comfort

When it comes to distractions, pain is a pretty effective one and probably comes near if not at the top of the list. It's like the one instrument in a band that is being played ten times louder than the others. Whilst you know there are other instruments, you have no chance of hearing what they're playing. To stay aware and present to what you're doing and how you're doing it, we explore our movements staying within our range of comfort. That doesn't mean we don't use some effort; after all, we're intentionally contracting our muscles. It means that we do that without moving into pain / burn / discomfort. I understand that some of you'll have been drawn to CSE because you're already in pain and / or feel constant discomfort, and perhaps there is no comfort zone right now. So how does this apply to you? My advice here is to explore your movements without moving into more discomfort or pain and without exacerbating your symptoms. To do this, you may start by just imagining doing the movements, simply motor planning them; I talked about this back in Chapter 6 The Science of Learning. You may also want to initially use a cushion or rolled up towel/ blanket under your head, or keep your knees bent rather than straightening them out whilst laying down.

- Slow down

We intentionally explore our movements slowly so that we can listen to the detail. When we feel the detail, we learn not only how we're moving but also where our SMA is showing up. When we feel this, we can learn to release it, reduce pain, and restore functional movement. As Hanna said, we cannot change what we cannot feel, and if we move too quickly, we miss the detail, the learning, and the opportunity to make long-term change. If you were to watch an action scene from a film in slow motion, imagine how much detail you would see in how the characters move and what they do, compared to if it were on fast forward. One of the ways our SMA shows up as we release out of a contraction is that the release feels bumpy, shaky, jerky, juddery. We notice this when we move slowly, it doesn't show up when we move too quickly. Think of your SMA as being akin to potholes in a road. If you speed over those potholes, you're unlikely to notice them, at least not until they have grown into huge holes. If you slow down, you'll feel more of them, which then opens an opportunity to fill in and heal those holes. In moving slowly, you gradually restore your brains control of your muscles, smoothing out the movements and restoring function.

- Less is more

I'm making an assumption here, but my guess is that you've probably spent a fair bit of your life working hard, and no wonder. From a young age, we're given innumerable messages about how if we're to succeed, achieve, be successful, be admired, and be accepted, we must work hard. "Working hard" is an admired trait, it's rewarded within our culture, and we place high value on how busy and productive we've been. How often do you feel guilty or have felt the need to justify being lazy, doing less, or apologise for not getting things done for fear of being stigmatised and frowned upon by others? Many of these messages are a cultural creation; so that means it's not written, and we could change our message, our story. Italian culture springs to mind here and makes me think of the wonderful Italian saying of *il dolce far niente*, the art and joy of doing nothing.

When it comes to our health and physicality, our culture is further reinforced through mantras such as "feel the burn" and "there's no gain without pain," "if it's hurting, it's working." Ugh! Call me innately lazy (and no, I'm not going to apologise for that!), but the concept of doing less to achieve change and growth feels way more appealing to me.

- Awareness, curiosity, and compassion

Bring these approaches to your practise and you'll always have something to learn and, therefore, the ability to create change. Awareness is the cornerstone of this practise; therefore, you'll be guided to notice what internal sensations you can or cannot feel as well as what you can and cannot feel from the outside in. When we're curious and kind to ourselves, there's no room for judgment. Judgment creates tension, which is held within our muscles. It isn't so much about "doing" the movements or doing them "right" or "wrong"; it's about having an opportunity to explore, learn, and create more space. When we explore and begin to release holding patterns, we find new movement opportunities. There are endless opportunities for increasing insight, creating change in how we function and feel, and freedom in how we think and live. These three approaches are fundamental factors to achieve this.

- Use your hands

The nature of SMA and your "normal" / habituated holding and movement patterns is that you struggle to feel them; they go unnoticed. Placing your hands on the areas you want to focus on, be that an area of lengthening or contracting, is like turning on a spotlight so that you can more clearly sense what is or isn't taking place. Using your hands to feel from the outside in, makes what you're doing more obvious and clearer to your brain. It increases your awareness and, therefore, ability to feel, learn, and create change.

- Video yourself

Aside from any potential cringing that seeing yourself on video might bring up, this is a seriously great way of expanding your learning and understanding of how you move and how your SMA shows up. When what we think we're doing is different from what we see we're doing, we know that chronic muscle tension is at play.

The three steps of pandiculation

Pandiculation has three specific steps much like a really satisfying yawn. They are:

- **Contract**: Tighten / shorten / contract your muscles more than they are
- **Release**: Slowly and with awareness, release the contraction all the way back to rest / no conscious effort
- **Rest**: Take a moment at rest to do nothing but breath and notice sensations before your next move. Pay attention to what a place of rest and release feels like. This may be unfamiliar territory, but we want to get really familiar with this place of release and rest. The more familiar and "normal" release and places of rest become, the easier it will be to find again.

CHAPTER SUMMARY

- ► How we do this practise is key.
- ► Soma scans are as important as the movements themselves.
- ► Minimise distractions.
- ► Try not to achieve anything by letting go of grasping at goals.
- ► Move within your range of comfort and avoid moving into or increasing pain and discomfort.
- ► Move slowly.
- ► Less is more.
- ► Explore with awareness, curiosity, and compassion.
- ► Use your hands.
- ► Follow the three steps of a pandiculation – contract, release, **rest.**

CHAPTER 11

The movements

The movements I have outlined for you in this book, are the start point to you moving towards more functional and freer movement. When explored as outlined above, these movements will help you to better understand *and* release your muscular holding patterns that have been contributing to your discomfort and restricted movement. Whilst there are innumerable ways of exploring the same movement patterns, and there are endless possibilities of movement combinations, I have outlined for you what I believe to be a solid foundation from which to grow and explore as your awareness and curiosity deepens. Every present moment is new; therefore, every time we come to our practise is a new moment full of new possibilities for freedom, autonomy, and control.

Soma scans

Whilst taking a scan, allow yourself to lie, stand, or sit in the laziest, easiest, and most comfortable way. Try to avoid and forget about feeling you need to hold yourself "correctly" or in a particular posture. This allows you to feel what your holding patterns are, and these are what you want to become familiar with, because your "normal" is where your chronic muscle tension lives.

There are many ways to take a soma scan and endless opportunities to notice and sense. Below is a guide to get you started with this, but don't allow it to restrict you. Get curious and allow your awareness to wander to what is showing up for you.

- Lying down scan

Lie comfortably on a firm surface, keeping knees bent if needed. Using your contact with the ground for feedback, notice:

- Where do you feel heaviest?
- Is there a part you're most aware of? If so, where and what do you sense there?
- Notice the imprint that your shoulder blades, rib cage and pelvis make through the left and right side. How balanced do you feel?
- Is one side heavier, flatter, bigger, more comfortable?
- Placing hands on your belly and chest, how much movement do you feel under your hands as you breath?
- Notice the imprint, weight, and shape of your heels. Do they feel equal? If your legs are straight, indulge in your curiosity and look at your feet. Are they pointing in the direction they felt like they were?

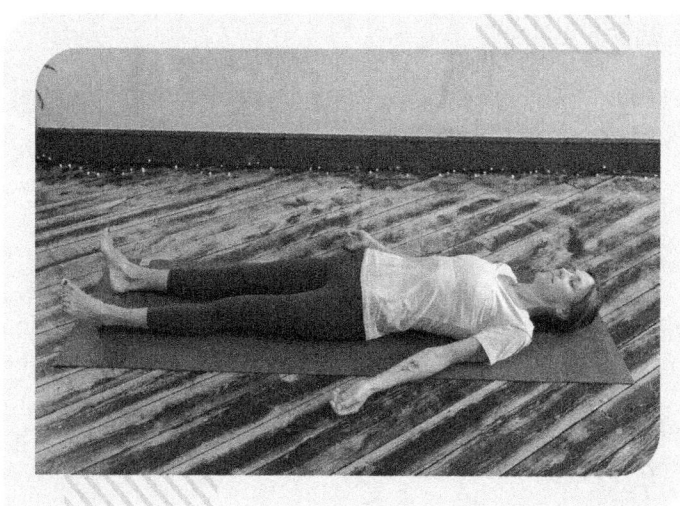

📝 NOTES & OBSERVATIONS

Freestyle pandiculation

Thanks to Colm McDonnell of www.learnsomatics.ie for sharing this brilliantly simple way of exploring pandiculation.

Reflex pattern – your unique pattern

Helps to – release tension / stress

This is a great way to start exploring the skill of pandiculating and intentionally releasing tension, without worrying about doing a particular movement.

Lying comfortably, go ahead and tighten anything and everything that feels okay to.

- Where do you notice tightening / contracting?

Slowly and with awareness release back to rest.

Repeat two or three more times:

- What shape do you make / scrunch into?
- Explore it again with half as much effort. Where do you feel tightening, then where do you feel relaxing and softening?

Repeat your soma scan and notice what and where changes occurred.

NOTES & OBSERVATIONS

Arch and flatten

These two movements are like our bread and butter. They help us begin to feel, release, and regain control of the big muscle groups in our centre. When we stop being able to relax and control the muscles around our waistline and pelvis, tightness and restrictions spread outwards from here through our entire system. Therefore, exploring these movements is a great place to start any practice.

NOTES & OBSERVATIONS

Arch and release

Reflex pattern – green light

Helps to – relieve lower back pain

This is one of the easiest and safest movements you can do to start relaxing and regaining control of your lower back muscles.

On your back with knees bent and feet roughly hip width and parallel, bring your focus to the back of your belt line and back of your pelvis. Notice the weight of your pelvis and how much space there is between your lower back and the mat. You could slide a hand under here to feel the space.

Contract - Begin to increase the arch of your lower back, lifting your belt line up away from the floor, tipping your pelvis towards your feet so the weight shifts towards your tailbone.

Release - Notice where you have arched and contracted your lower back muscles, then intentionally release out of this to rest, letting the pelvis roll back as you lengthen and soften your lower back muscles.

Rest – Notice how your lower back has lengthened and softened.

Repeat the three steps:

- Allow your belly to lengthen and expand as your lower back arches.
- Notice if your head moves; if not, bring it in intentionally by dropping your chin down following the direction of your pubic bones. These are located at the front centre of your pelvis, in between the tops of your legs.

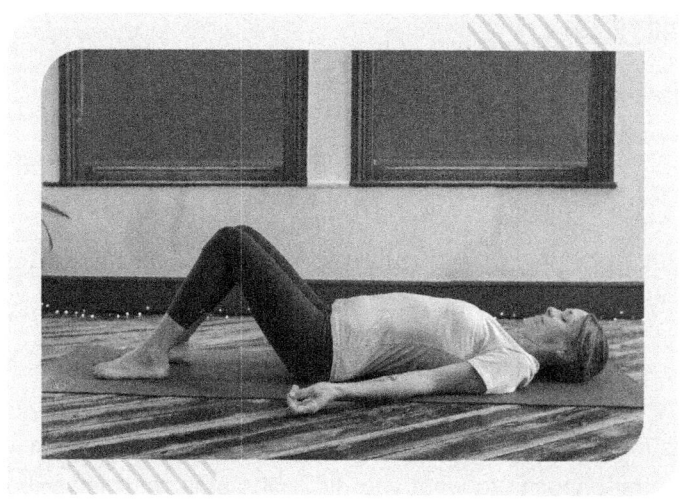

 NOTES & OBSERVATIONS

Flatten and release

Reflex pattern – red light

Helps to - release tension through the belly including digestive issues, feelings of worry / fear / anxiety, neck pain. Increases fuller and freer breathing.

This movement helps you to feel the lengthening of your lower back as you intentionally tighten then release the muscles of your belly.

Contract - In the same start position as for the arch and release, flatten and sink your lower back towards the floor as you sink and tighten your belly. Let your pelvis roll, tipping your pubic bone upwards towards your navel. Notice how this is the opposite to what you did in the arch. Your lower back is now lengthening and your front is shortening and sinking.

Release – Slowly release the tightening of your belly, letting it soften and lengthen back to rest. Allow your lower back and pelvis to passively follow along with the release of your belly.

Rest – Take a moment at rest to feel your belly soft and open and the small curve of your lower back return.

Repeat the three steps:

- As you release through the front, allow the back to follow passively. Notice if you push or arch your back as you release your belly.
- Notice if your head moves as you flatten. If it doesn't, intentionally tip your head back, shortening the back of the neck with your chin tipping towards the ceiling.
- Notice if your neck releases as you lengthen and relax your belly. If it doesn't happen freely, intentionally lengthen the back of your neck to a resting length.

 **NOTES & OBSERVATIONS**

Rebalancing the pelvis

Reflex pattern – Trauma reflex

Helps to – Relieve one sided back pain, Sacroiliac (SI) joint discomfort

Our holding patterns, including any rotation or tipping to one side through our centre will show up in our arch and flatten. To find our true centre and release any rotation or imbalance requires us to first notice where this may be happening. This movement helps you to find your true centre and relieve one-sided discomfort around your lower back and pelvis.

Contract – Arch your lower back (as above) and notice if you tip more into one side of your pelvis, or one side of your lower back feels tighter. Go ahead and intentionally arch off centre, tipping more into that side that feels heavier or tighter. Let your head follow.

Release – Slowly release the tightening of your lower back, letting it soften and lengthen. Let your pelvis release back to centre, your head too.

Rest – Take a moment at rest to feel the balance of your pelvis and the resting length of your back muscles.

Repeat the above arch off centre, two or three times on each side:

- Notice how your head follows. Does it also roll slightly off centre?
- As you arch your back and roll your pelvis off centre, gently press your opposite shoulder blade back into the floor, like a diagonal arch across the back of your torso.

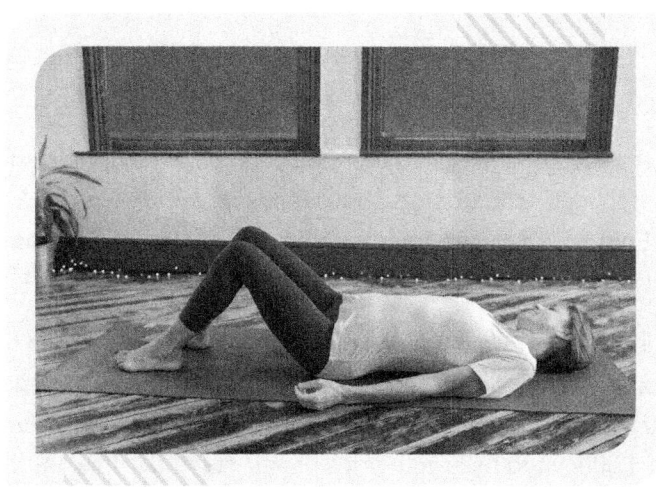

NOTES & OBSERVATIONS

Flower

Reflex pattern – primarily the red light reflex

Helps to – Relieve shoulder pain, rounded shoulder / stooped posture, digestive issues, feelings around worry/fear/sadness/withdrawn, neck pain, midback pain. Enables fuller and freer breathing and increases coordination and balance between the front and back of your torso.

The flower is a great movement for being able to release and open out through your front, and it helps us to feel the connection between our centre and our limbs. If you spend a lot of time hunched over a desk, sitting in a slumped position, or find it difficult to raise your arms or sit / stand tall, this one is for you.

Contract – Belly, chest, front of shoulders, back of neck. Sink and tighten your belly, flattening your back. Sink your chest / breastbone down towards the floor as you roll your shoulders forward, lifting your shoulder blades away from the floor and tip your head back. Roll your arms, like rolling pins, in to hug the sides of your torso, with your palms facing out.

You're recreating the red light / startle reflex pattern.

Release – Slowly begin to soften and release your belly. Let that release continue up through your chest, across your shoulders, through your neck and down your arms to your fingertips. Let your arms rest wherever they roll to.

Rest – Take a moment to notice the space through your front and the movement as you breath freely.

Repeat, and this time as you flatten and sink through your front, bring your legs into it by tipping your knees together. Notice what tightens from your belly down through your inner thighs.

When we have released some of the holding tension through our front, we're then able to lengthen and explore the opposite movement part of the flower.

Contract – Arch your lower back, lengthening your belly and tipping head and pubic bones towards your feet. Press your shoulder blades back into the floor and notice how this affects your arms. Like rolling pins, roll your arms away from your sides creating space between your sides and arms.

Release – Slowly release the arch of your back, allow your shoulder blades to soften and widen, let your arms release and come to rest wherever they land.

Rest – Take a moment to notice the length, width, and softness through your back.

Repeat the above, and, this time, let your legs join in. As you arch and contract the muscles up through your back, tip your knees outwards like your arms, and notice what lengthens through your front from your chest down to your inner thighs.

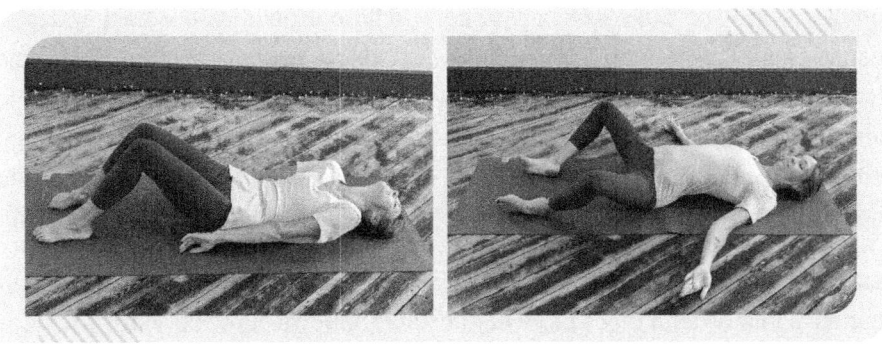

✎ NOTES & OBSERVATIONS

Baby back lift

Reflex pattern – Green light

Helps to – Relieve back pain, easier bending forward, connect the movement of your head with the length of your spine.

The baby back lift is a great way to feel the connection between our back muscles and our head, as well as finding relief by learning how to relax these muscles that are often held tight. This movement is something that we started to do when we were around 3 months old and is known as the Landau reflex. Laid on our round soft belly, we would begin to lift our head as our back muscles contracted, allowing us to look around and explore our environment. To be able to do this with ease and in a functional way, we need to be able to lengthen and let go of our belly and chest. As you explore this movement and think about contracting your back muscles, check that you're letting go of your belly and not holding it in. See if you can allow it to be heavy into the floor.

Lie on your front, place your forehead on the back of your hands, or take your hands a little wider if that's more comfortable, elbows out wide. Have your legs roughly hip width apart.

Contract – Lengthen your belly, press the front of your pelvis into the floor as you sink and contract your lower back and glute muscles. Keep lengthening in the front, from your belly up through your chest and lift your head. You can send every inhale into your front to help with the lengthening here.

Release – Slowly soften and lengthen your back muscles, notice how your head begins to lower.

Rest – Take a moment at rest to feel and check that your back muscles and glutes have released. This may happen after you have finished moving, so take your time to listen beyond the end of the movement.

✎ NOTES & OBSERVATIONS

Back lift

Reflex pattern – Green light

Helps to – Relieve back pain, enables easier bending forward, improve walking and balance,

Whilst the baby back lift is more an exploration of spinal extension, this version of back lift explores the rotational pattern that takes place when we walk in a functional way. It helps us to increase control and connection of the muscles across our diagonals between shoulders and opposite hips. Maintaining awareness and control of these functional diagonal patterns enables us to continue walking in a balanced, coordinated, and functional way. Whichever version of back lift you're exploring, they're essential movements for helping us to relax and regain control of our back muscles, so that we can move more comfortably and do necessary actions such as bending over to pick something up or to put socks on. Whichever side you start on, be sure to also explore this on the second side.

Your start position is lying on your front with your head turned to one side. Place your same side hand palm down in front of your face, with your elbow out to the side away from your ribs. Your other arm can rest down by your side. I'll first break down each part of this movement.

Contract – Lift up your elbow and notice what you feel contracting around the top and back of your shoulder.

Release – Slowly lower your elbow, paying attention to any bumps or shakes along the way.

Rest – Let the elbow rest and notice how your shoulder settles.

For the second part of this pattern leave your elbow on the ground and:

Contract – Sink and contract your lower back as you let your belly and chest expand, and lift up your head, as if light as a feather. Notice where you feel the effort through your back. Is it your upper back, lower back and / or maybe your glute muscles?

Release – Slowly soften and lengthen your back to lower your head.

Rest – Notice what lets go in your back.

If lifting the head on its own feels enough for you, then stay with that. Alternatively, you can now connect the back of your fingers with your floor side cheek and:

Contract – Plant your pelvis into the floor and as you lengthen your belly and chest, let your elbow, hand, and head float up. Pause at the top of the movement to notice what parts of your back you feel working / contracting.

Release – Focusing upon your back, slowly release and lengthen to lower your elbow, hand, and head.

Rest – Notice if there is more release at rest, even after you've finished moving.

Repeat the above steps and this time:

Contract - Lengthen your opposite leg and allow it to lift up if comfortable. Notice a shortening across the back of this diagonal and a lengthening across the front.

Release – As you lower, sense a lengthening across the back as the muscles soften and release.

Rest – Notice how your back feels to have released.

Repeat these movements on the other side.

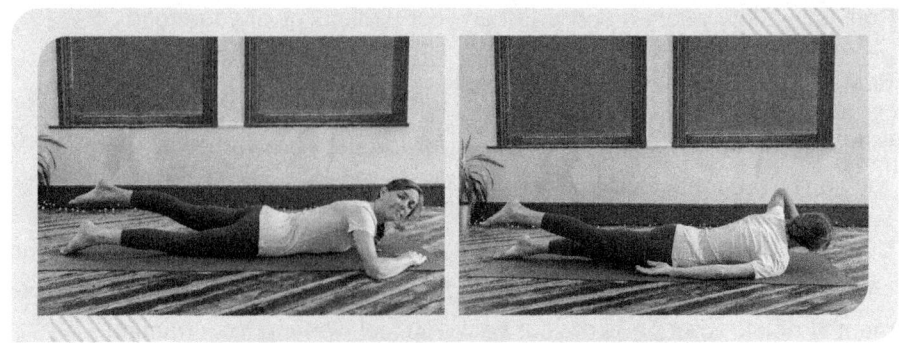

✎ NOTES & OBSERVATIONS

Arch and Curl

Reflex pattern – Primarily the red light reflex

Helps to – Relieve mid back pain, increase easier and fuller breathing, relieve neck pain, enables easier lifting of your arms, easier and more comfortable to sit and stand tall, relieve rounded shoulder posture.

Whilst this may look very similar to a sit-up or crunch exercise, the intention of this movement is very different and not to be confused with any desired attempt to gain yourself a six pack. Exploring this movement after the back lift really gives you an opportunity to feel how freely and comfortably your back muscles can lengthen. And, whilst there is effort through the muscles of your front, this is a sinking and shortening of your front, coordinated with a lengthening and letting go of your back, rather than a bracing. Your ability to curl up here is dependent upon your ability to comfortably lengthen your back. Therefore, this movement is all about the relationship and coordination between the muscles of your front and your back.

Lie on your back, knees bent and feet roughly hip width apart; interlink your fingers and place your head in the palms of your hands. If your elbows are raised off the floor, support them with blankets or cushions so that they can be heavy and resting.

Contract – Arch your back pressing your tailbone and head back into the floor. Check that you're letting your belly and chest lengthen and widen.

Release – Focusing on the effort through your back, slowly let your arch soften and lengthen back to rest.

Rest – Take a moment at rest to check that you have let your back release and that your belly is soft and not pulled in.

Now begin to sink your lower back down and lift your elbows up and towards each other. Notice how your back lengthens and widens.

Contract – As your back lengthens, begin to sink your belly and chest as you lift your head and shoulders forward. Only go as far as you feel your back lengthen comfortably without force or stretch. If you feel shaking, make the range of movement smaller.

Release – Keeping your elbows up and towards each other, slowly lengthen your front, creating space between your pubic bones and your chest. When your head lands take another breath or two to slowly release your chest muscles to unfold your elbows. Notice any shaky, jumpy, bumpy movements on the release.

At rest, take a moment to notice the space and breath through your front. Notice if your back contracted and arched when you released your front. If so, could you also let that release too.

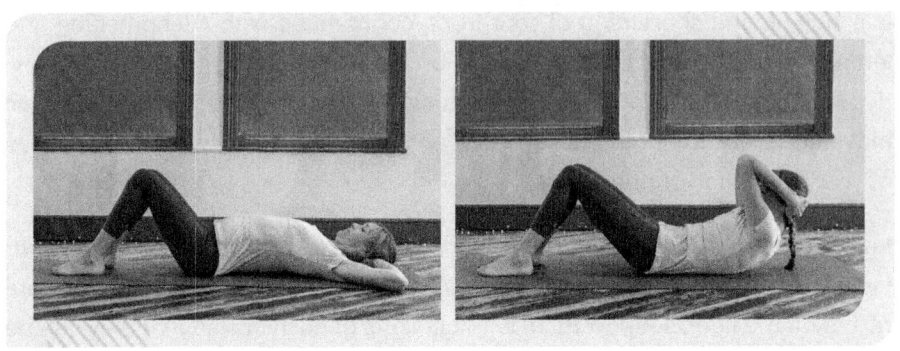

✎ NOTES & OBSERVATIONS

Arch and diagonal curl

Reflex pattern – Primarily the red light reflex

Helps to – As arch and curl but through the diagonals. Increase connection, control, and coordination between shoulders and opposite hips. Increase balanced and coordinated walking.

Knees bent and roughly hip width apart, place the palm of one hand behind your head, supporting the elbow as needed. This will be the shoulder / diagonal that you start with. To bring awareness to this diagonal, use your other hand to trace across from the front of the shoulder over to the opposite hip.

Contract – Gently arch your back pressing the focus shoulder blade and elbow gently into the floor. Feel how your front has to lengthen to do this comfortably.

Release – Slowly and with awareness release your back and any pressing.

Rest -Check that your front and back are released.

Contract – Begin to flatten your lower back and widen your upper back as you lift and fold your elbow in. Lift your opposite knee towards its same side shoulder. Keep lengthening your back as you sink and shorten your front, curling up and then turning towards your opposite knee. You're curling on the diagonal. Feel how your front shortens and your back lengthens here.

Release – Slowly begin to release and lengthen from your hip crease, across your belly and chest to the opposite shoulder. Once your foot and head have landed, take another breath or two to slowly lower the elbow.

Rest – Check if your back is still soft and your front is long. After several repetitions on this side, take time for a scan before your second side and compare the effects of before and after. Does your first side feel longer, clearer, or perhaps more connected?

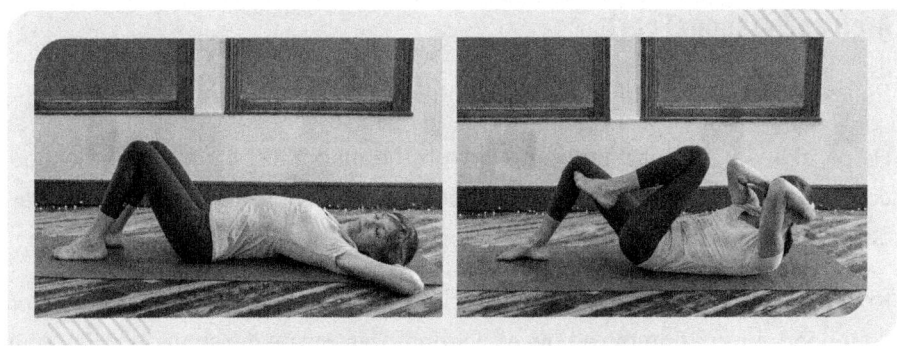

📝 NOTES & OBSERVATIONS

Side bend

Reflex pattern – Trauma reflex

Helps to – Release one sided discomfort, pain and restricted movement through the pelvis and hips, knees and feet, shoulders and neck. Increase balance and coordination of movement and function between left and right. Restore equal resting length through our sides and balance misalignments through pelvis, shoulders, and neck. Reduce apparent leg length discrepancy.

The side bend is all about increasing awareness and control of the muscles that connect our front with our back. To ensure we're exploring the movement through our sides, our set up is key here. It can help to lay in front of a wall or sofa so that you have some feedback behind you and a clearer sense of where you are in space. You'll explore this movement on both sides, though if you're more comfortable lying on one side, I recommend you start by lying on that side first.

Lying on your side, if comfortable, rest your head on your floor, side arm laid out long; otherwise, use a cushion or blanket to rest your head comfortably. Have your legs together with your hips and knees bent at 90-degree angles. If lying on a mat, use the front and back edges to line up your spine, the back of your pelvis, head, and shins. With your top hand, bring your awareness to your top side by tracing up and down between your armpit and the side of your hip joint, noticing the length and changes in texture from your ribs, past your waist to your pelvis. Notice the spaces in between your ribs.

Firstly, let's explore the hip end of this movement:

Contract - Take a hold of your waist with your top hand and hike your hip towards it in the direction of your armpit, intentionally shortening the space between the side of your pelvis and side of your ribcage. Allow your top foot to float up in the direction of the ceiling, in response to hiking your hip. Pause in the movement and notice the contraction of your waist muscles.

Release – Slowly lengthen your waist releasing your hip and notice the change in space and texture of your waist.

Rest – Check that your waist has softened, and your hip and foot are rested.

Let's now explore the rib end of this movement:

Contract – Lay your top arm along your side, with your fingertips pointing in the direction of the bottom end of your mat. Slide your armpit towards your waist, closing the space in between the side of each rib as you do. Allow your top side shoulder to follow and your head to lift and follow too. Feel where you have shortened and tightened along this top side.

Release – From your waist, slowly begin to lengthen this side, creating space from your waist, between each rib and all the way up into your armpit. Allow the shoulder and head to come back to a resting spot.

Rest – Take a moment to feel the space and movement as you breath freely along this top side.

Now let's bring these two ends together for the full side bend. This movement is much like playing your side like an accordion. Think of your armpit and side of your hip as the handles being drawn towards each other, then slowly moving away from each other.

As you come into your side bend, notice if you feel the floor side of your torso lengthen as you shorten along the top.

Notice where you feel the contraction and tightening as you move into your side bend. Is it through your side, or do you notice your back or belly tightening?

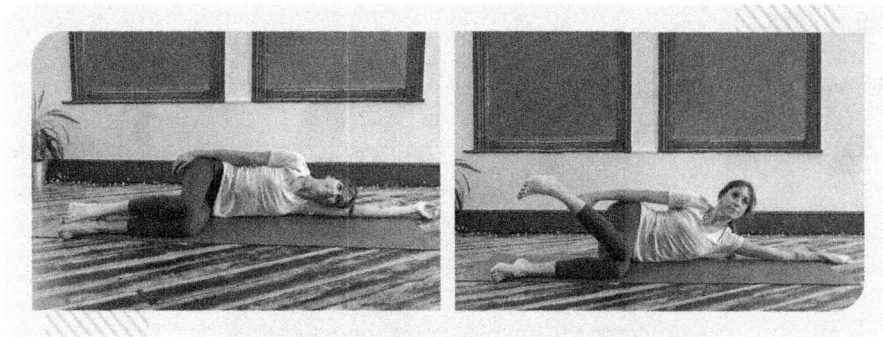

📝 **NOTES & OBSERVATIONS**

Hip Hikers

Reflex pattern – Trauma reflex

Helps to - Release one-sided discomfort, pain, and restricted movement, especially through the pelvis, hips, knees, and feet. Increases balance and equality of movement and function between left and right. Restores equal length through your waist.

This movement is similar to the hip hike you experienced on your side in the side bend, but here you explore the movement lying on your back with your knees bent and roughly hip width apart. Using your hands to help feel the movement, take ahold of your waist at the side, so that your thumbs wrap around the back and your fingertips wrap around your front pointing in the direction of your navel.

Contract - Hike one side of your pelvis towards your waist, as if you need to balance a wash basket on your hip. Notice the change of space and texture at your waist. Has it shortened and contracted?

Release – Slowly create space at your waist, releasing your hip back to a place of no conscious effort.

Rest - Notice how the space and texture of your waist has changed. How even in length do the two sides of your waist feel at rest?

Repeat this movement three or four times on each side. As you hike and intentionally shorten one side, notice if and how the opposite waist lengthens. Where we have more unconscious holding tension in the muscles of one side, we may find this movement is easier and more coordinated than the other.

As with the side bend, notice where you feel the effort in this movement. Do you notice your back arching as you attempt to hike your hip? Our back muscles can perform well in doing the effort of our waist muscles if we have forgotten how to control them. If you notice your back arching, do an arch and release first to relax and lengthen your lower back muscles, then explore another hip hike.

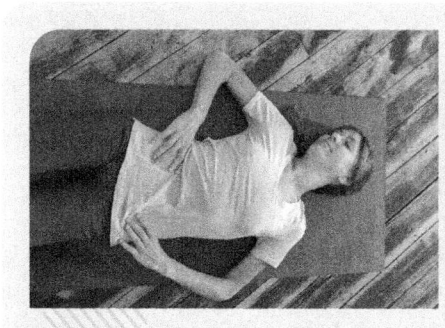 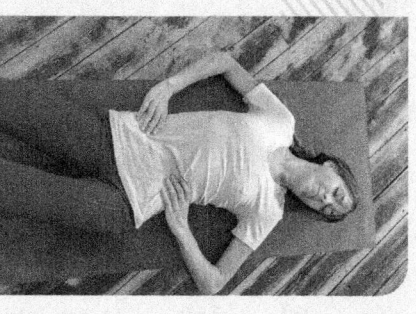

NOTES & OBSERVATIONS

Washrag

Reflex pattern – This is an integrative movement and not a pandiculation as you have explored in the above movements.

Helps to – Relieve tension around the shoulders and neck.

This movement helps us to feel and restore a full soma rotation from our crown to our toes, and across our shoulders from one hand to the other. Maintaining our ability to rotate our spine is an essential function to be able to walk and run with ease and efficiency. Functional rotation is also essential for our safety, enabling us to direct our senses of sight, smell, and hearing. Furthermore, restoring these movement patterns makes everyday actions such as crossing the road, riding a bike, or driving and parking a car not only safer but also more comfortable.

To prepare for your washrag, lie on your back, knees bent and maybe a little wider than hip width. Place your arms out wide from your sides, almost but not quite at a full T position.

Let's start with the upper part of this movement:

- Notice your shoulder blades in contact with the floor. Begin to press one shoulder blade back into the floor and rotate the arm on that side so the palm faces the ceiling. Let your head roll towards that shoulder and feel the connection of the muscles of your neck and the back of this shoulder.
- At the same time, do the opposite with your other shoulder and arm. Peel your other shoulder blade away from the floor, rolling it forward, and rotate this arm so that your palm rolls in the direction of the floor.
- Keeping your elbows soft so as not to strain, allow your arms to rotate in their opposite directions just as far as is comfortable. Alternate from side to side, sensing where your centre is as you meet and pass through it.

Now let's explore the lower part of this movement:

- Begin to tip your pelvis to one side, left or right, letting the knees tip with it and allowing the soles of the feet to roll. Roll your head in the opposite direction.
- Feel how the opposite side of your waist to where your knees are tipping lengthens.

- Alternate from side to side, sensing where your centre is as you meet and pass through it.

Now let's explore adding the upper and lower parts together:

- As you tip your pelvis and legs to one side, roll the same side shoulder forward away from the floor, and the opposite shoulder back into the floor. Rotate the arms as above and roll the head towards the shoulder pressing back / opposite direction to the knees.
- Notice how you're rotating from your head to your toes, and from your right to your left across your shoulders.

See if you can explore this movement in a lazy and indulgent way, as if it were the most luxurious movement that you could possibly do.

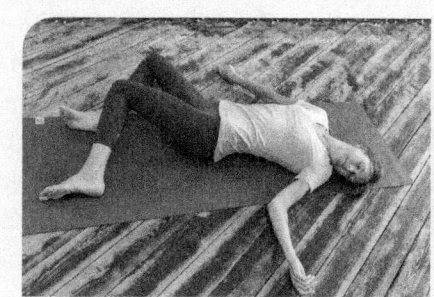 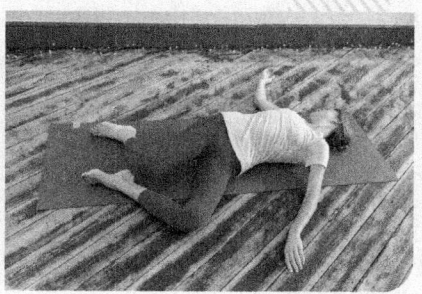

NOTES & OBSERVATIONS

CHAPTER 12

Seated and standing movements

Where and in what positions do you spend most of your time? I'm guessing your answer is unlikely to be *lying on the floor*, but perhaps it's standing on your feet or sitting on the sofa, in a car, or at a desk. For these reasons I have included movements that you can explore standing and sitting, making this practice accessible no matter your mobility options or where you are. It may also be that getting up and down from the floor isn't comfortable for you right now. Or, perhaps your environment doesn't offer you the space to lie down. Having options for where and how you can do your practice means you're more likely to be able to integrate this into your everyday life, creating your own somatic habit.

Seated movements

- Seated scan

Sitting in a firm chair, sit towards the front edge of your seat with the soles of your feet in contact with the ground. Notice the weight through your sit bones in contact with the seat of your chair:

- Does one sit bone feel heavier or more comfortable?
- Do your knees look level?
- How balanced do your footprints feel?
- Where does your gaze land?

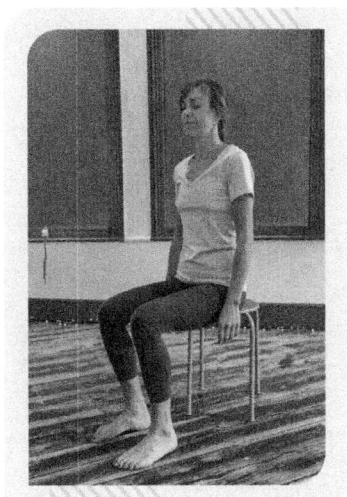

NOTES & OBSERVATIONS

Freestyle pandiculation

Reflex pattern – your unique pattern

Helps to – release tension / stress

This is a great place to start exploring your practise and feel how it is to pandiculate without worrying about doing a particular movement. It also helps to notice where you're holding yourself in this moment.

Start by sitting or standing in the easiest most comfortable way, then go ahead and tighten anything and everything that feels okay to. Allow yourself to sink and tighten into where you're drawn and whatever position feels easy, perhaps familiar.

Where do you notice tightening / contracting?

Slowly and with awareness release back to rest.

Repeat two or three more times:

- What shape do you make / scrunch into?
- Explore it again with half as much effort. Where do you notice tightening / shortening?

Repeat your soma scan and notice what changes occurred.

NOTES & OBSERVATIONS

Arch and release

Reflex pattern – Green light reflex

Helps to – Relax the muscles and ease discomfort and tension through your lower back.

After taking your soma scan, begin to shift your weight forward of your sit bones, tipping your pubic bones down towards the floor between your thighs. Let your tail bone swing up and back towards the rear of your chair. You're rolling your pelvis forward, increasing the curve of your lower back.

Contract – Feel your lower back arch more as you contract your muscles here. Allow your belly to expand forward and your chin tip down towards your chest.

Release – Focus on the arch and effort through your lower back, and slowly soften and lengthen these muscles back to a place of no conscious effort.

Rest – Take a moment at rest and feel how your lower back has softened, the arch has reduced, and notice how your weight returns more towards the top of your sit bones.

Repeat two or three times.

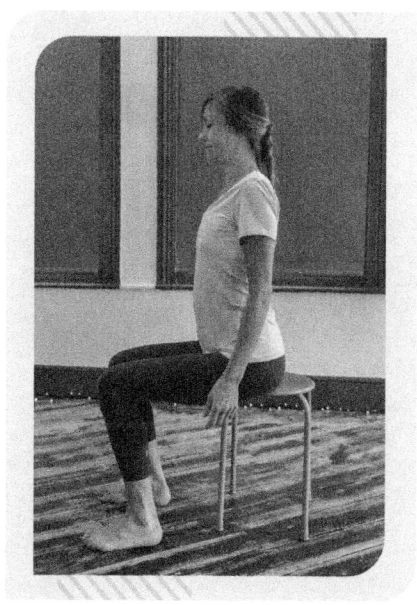

NOTES & OBSERVATIONS

Flatten and release

Reflex pattern – Red light reflex

Helps to - Release tightness through tummy and chest muscles. Eases mid back pain. Increases ability to breath more fully. Releases rounded shoulder / slumped posture and helps us to more easily sit up tall with less effort.

After taking your soma scan, begin to shift your weight towards the back of your sit bones, as if rolling your pelvis like a ball. Allow your lower back to round and lengthen as you sink and tighten your belly. Tip your pubic bones up in the direction of your navel and let your head move forward as you tip your chin up towards the ceiling.

Contract – Intentionally tighten your belly, sinking your navel back towards your spine. Let your chest sink a little as well. Notice how the front of your torso and the back of your neck shorten and tighten.

Release – Slowly and with awareness begin to soften your belly, letting it lengthen back to a resting spot. Let the back of your neck lengthen as well.

Rest – Take a moment to notice the space from your pubic bones up to your chest, and the weight back on top of your sit bones.

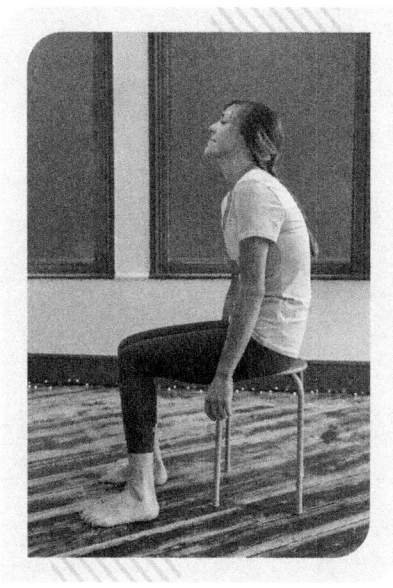

📝 NOTES & OBSERVATIONS

Arch and flatten

To feel the relationship, connection, and coordination between your front and back, explore the two movements described above together. Be sure to take a moment in between them to feel where your place of rest is. Notice if one of these movements feels more familiar or easier.

NOTES & OBSERVATIONS

Flower

Reflex pattern – primarily red light

Helps to – Relieve shoulder pain, rounded shoulder / stooped posture, digestive issues, feelings around worry/fear/sadness/withdrawn, neck pain, mid-back pain. Enables fuller and freer breathing.

The flower is a great movement for being able to release and open out through your front, and it helps us to feel the connection between and coordination of our centre and our limbs. If you spend a lot of time hunched over a desk, this is a great movement snack that you can take without even leaving your chair.

With your feet planted on the ground and arms resting down by your sides, begin to flatten and round your back, tipping your pubic bones towards your navel and drawing your belly back towards your spine. As you sink your chest let your head tip up and roll your shoulders forward as if to slump, rolling your arms in towards your sides. Bring your legs into the pattern by pressing your knees together and rolling to the inside edges of your feet.

Contract – Feel where you have tightened through your front, inner thighs, and back of neck.

Release – Slowly begin to release the effort through your front, from your centre up through your chest, neck shoulders and arms, and down through your inner thighs all the way to your feet.

Rest – Notice what space you have created through your front, and the ease with which you can breath and sit tall.

Contract – Now arching your lower back, rolling your pubic bones forwards and down towards the floor. Draw your shoulder blades back opening your chest and roll your arms out away from your sides. Bring your legs into the pattern by tipping your knees outwards and rolling towards the outside edges of your feet.

Release – Feel where the effort is through your back, and from the centre of your back, begin to release the effort in all directions.

Rest – Notice how it feels to sit at rest with no conscious effort through your back.

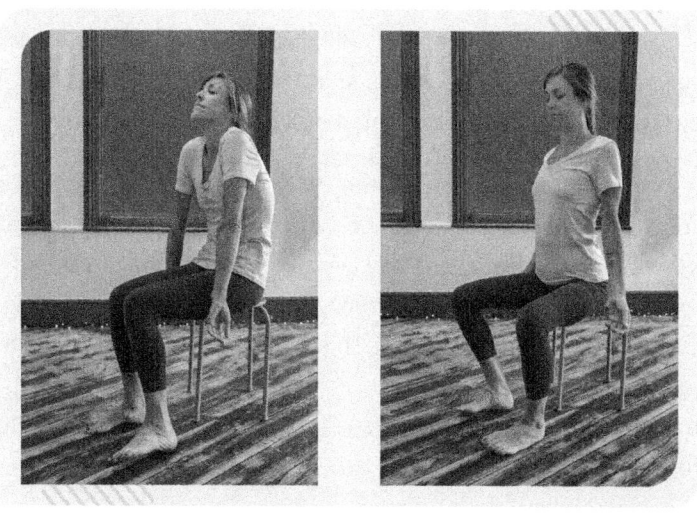

NOTES & OBSERVATIONS

Side bend

Reflex pattern – Trauma reflex

Helps to – release one sided tension and holding patterns to find our true centre. Relieves one-sided pain, such as shoulder, neck, hip, and knee. Balances uneven shoulders, head tilts, and apparent leg length discrepancy.

Noticing your contact with your seat, do you feel more weight or contact through one sit bone. Also notice the contact that your feet make with the ground. How balanced do they feel? Using your hands, trace up and down the sides of your torso one at a time, from your armpits, along the sides of your ribcage, your waist and your pelvis. This is where you'll be doing the movement and, therefore, where you want to focus your attention. Choose which side you'd like to start with, and we shall begin with exploring the upper / rib part of this movement:

Contract - Slide your armpit straight down towards your waist, in the direction of the ground. Notice how the space between your ribs and the length of your side shortens. Allow the same side shoulder and your head to follow.

Release – From the side of your waist, slowly and with awareness begin to lengthen back up through your ribs, to your armpit, shoulder, neck, and head.

Rest – Notice how your side has lengthened and your head is back on top of your spine. Take a moment to notice the space through this side.

Now for the hip part of this movement. Imagine there is a drawing pin under the same side sit bone. Begin to lift your hip up towards your same side armpit, in the direction of the ceiling.

Contract - Notice how your waist contracts and shortens to hike your hip upwards, and the space between the side of your pelvis and ribcage shortens.

Release – From the side of your waist, slowly begin to lengthen and create space between the side of your pelvis and ribcage, relaxing your waist muscles and releasing your hip and sit bone back to rest.

Rest- Take a moment at rest to feel the space at your waist and the weight through your sit bone.

Now put these two ends together, rib end and hip end, for the full side bend.

Contract – Send your armpit towards your waist, letting the shoulder, arm, and head follow, as your hike your hip up towards your armpit. Feel your side shorten like an accordion.

Release – Slowly from your waist begin to release in both directions, relaxing and lengthening your muscles as you go.

Rest – Feel how your side has opened and lengthened and where your head and gaze return to. Take a moment to feel the space and breath through this side.

Repeat three or four times on this side and notice how freely your opposite side lengthens as you side bend. Does the opposite sit bone get heavier? Can you sense more space between your ribs on your lengthening side?

Before switching sides, take a moment at rest to feel the effects of this side bend through your first side. Is there a different sense of space, length, or movement as you breathe, compared with the side you've not yet pandiculated?

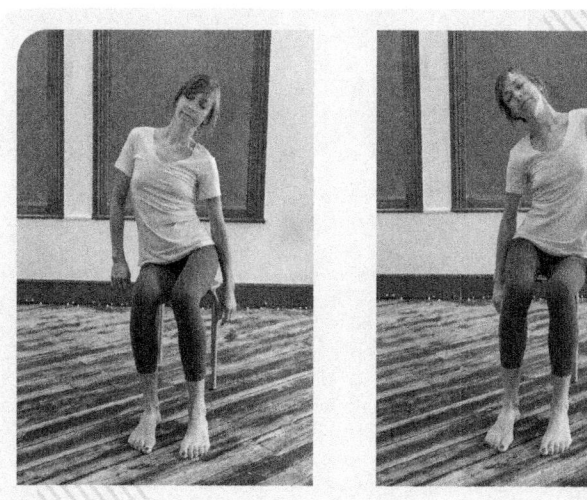

📝 NOTES & OBSERVATIONS

Standing movements

As with the seated movements described above, exploring these movements in standing gives us even more opportunities to be present and continue releasing stress throughout our day, no matter where we are. Waiting in a queue, for the kettle to boil, or even pausing during a dog walk, I find myself moving and pandiculating!

- Standing scan

Using the ground for feedback, notice and compare your footprints.

 Some questions to consider

- Do you feel more weight through one foot?
- How much of each foot do you feel in contact with the floor?
- Where do you feel the most weight through each foot – ball, heel, an edge?

Bring your awareness up through your soma and consider:

- Does one leg feel more active, have more energy through it, like it's supporting you more?
- What do you feel through your knees and hips?
- Are you more aware of your front or your back?
- Where is your gaze?
- How comfortable is it for you to stand here?

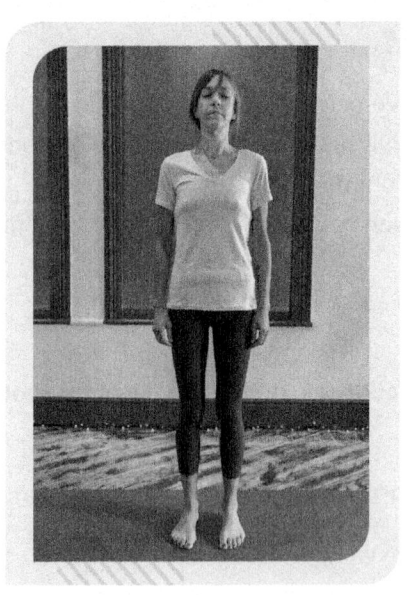

NOTES & OBSERVATIONS

Freestyle pandiculation -exaggerate your pattern.

This is a great way to become more aware of how you're holding yourself in space. By doing more of what you're already doing, you're becoming aware of what your "normal" is. It's like putting a spotlight on it. Do this by:

- Shift more weight into the foot, or areas of your feet where you feel the most weight.
- Stand even more into the leg that has more weight / energy going through it / is supporting you more.
- If you notice you're looking more towards the floor or ceiling, shift your gaze and head even more in the direction of where your gaze lands.
- Slowly release out of your exaggeration and notice what happens to your sense of balance and comfort.

Repeat two or three times, and then notice if your resting standing position has shifted in any way.

Mirror image:

Standing in front of a mirror is another great way of exploring and becoming more aware of asymmetries and how we unconsciously hold ourselves. In particular, it can help us to see how the trauma reflex may be showing up for us with one-sided tightness and rotations.

Standing in front of a mirror, close your eyes and let yourself settle into the easiest most normal and comfortable way of standing, allowing your arms to hang as they want to and one or both knees bending if they want to.

Open your eyes and notice:

- How level are the tops of your shoulders?
- Is your head centered or tipping / positioned more to one side?
- Where do your fingertips land and are they level?
- Is one arm, shoulder, hip or leg, further forward towards the mirror than the other?

Based upon what you can see and feel, go ahead and exaggerate that and notice:

- Where do you sink / shorten?

- Where do you lengthen?
- Where has the weight shifted through your legs and feet?
- Has this increased your sense of tension in certain areas?

Repeat this two or three times, then explore the opposite to that pattern. If you were sinking one arm and shoulder down, switch and do that with the other shoulder / arm. Does it feel as easy and normal when you explore a similar pattern through the opposite side?

NOTES & OBSERVATIONS

Arch and release

Reflex pattern – Green light reflex

Helps to – Relax the muscles and ease discomfort and tension through your lower back. Allows you to bend forward with ease.

Imagine you've just been told to stand up straight! Starting at your feet, begin to turn your toes slightly outward, shifting the weight forward towards the balls of your feet and straighten your legs. Let your belly move forward as you increase the arch of your lower back, feeling like you stick your bum out a little. Draw your shoulders back, letting your arms move with them. Let your chin drop down keeping your gaze forward.

Contract – Feel an intentional tightening of the muscles from your lower back up to your shoulder blades.

Release – Slowly and intentionally soften the arch of your lower back, allow your shoulder blades to widen, let your knees soften, let the weight shift back towards the centre of your feet.

Rest – Take a moment after releasing out of this green light reflex to notice the length and comfort through your back.

Repeat two or three times, then take time to scan and notice where the weight is through your feet.

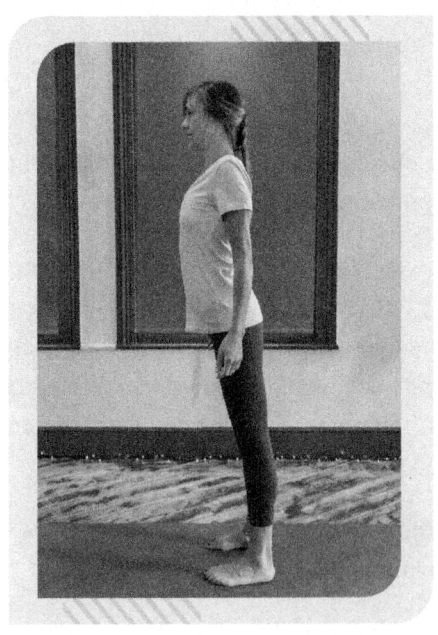

✎ NOTES & OBSERVATIONS

Flatten and release

Reflex pattern – The red light reflex

Helps to – Relieve mid back pain, increase easier and fuller breathing, relieve neck pain, enables easier lifting of your arms, easier and more comfortable to sit and stand tall, relieve rounded shoulder posture.

When we hold tightness through our chest and tummy, just being able to stand up can feel challenging and even exhausting. Sinking further into this pattern of the red light reflex enables us to lengthen and release so that we can just stand more easily.

Imagine (you may not have to!) that you have no energy to stay upright. Tighten your belly and sink your chest, rounding your shoulders forward as you do, letting your arms follow. This may be a familiar position if you spend time slumped over a laptop or book. Lift your chin and let your head move slightly forward, as if you were looking at your computer screen. Feel your back rounding. Bend your knees towards each other, pointing your toes inward a little. Sink into your heels and towards the inside edges of your feet.

Contract – Intentionally tighten your belly and chest, maybe even your inner thighs.

Release – Slowly soften your belly and chest as you lengthen from your pubic bones up towards your chest and shoulders. Straighten your legs and feel the weight shift back through your feet.

Rest – Take a moment at rest and notice the space through your front and your comfort in being able to stand.

Repeat two or three times, then notice where you feel the weight through your feet, where your gaze lands and how comfortable you feel in standing. Do you feel more upright?

✏️ NOTES & OBSERVATIONS

Back lift

Reflex – Green light

Helps to – Relax your back muscles to reduce back pain and increase ability to bend over with ease. Release tension headaches and restore functional walking by helping us to remember our unique bipedal motion and the connection between shoulders and opposite hips.

Start by taking a walk around your space and pause midstride with one leg forward of the other, as if you were playing a game of musical statues and the music just stopped. The leg that is forward, notice where your same side arm and shoulder are. Is the arm swinging forward with the leg, swinging backward or somewhere in between? Perhaps it's still by your side. Where does your gaze land? Is it directly forward or slightly off centre? Notice your balance whilst paused. Do you feel grounded or as if you're about to topple? Keep walking and pause to compare the opposite side with your other leg forward.

In standing, take a step forward with one leg as if you were about to walk and let the same side shoulder and arm swing slightly backward. Allow your head to turn slightly towards that shoulder. Notice the back of this diagonal from the shoulder blade across to the opposite buttock and leg; they're both swinging backwards. Notice how the front of this diagonal lengthens. Switch and compare with the other diagonal and notice if one feels more coordinated or balanced than the other.

Let's explore this pattern in a different way, which you did in the laying down version of the back lift described earlier.

Step forward with one leg and bring the same side fingertips to your opposite cheek. With the back of your fingers to the opposite cheek, lift your elbow so it's roughly level with the top of your shoulder.

Keeping hand and face connected, turn your elbow and head to look to the side, allowing your upper back to rotate and notice:

Contract – Feel what tightens and works across the back of this diagonal, from the shoulder that is turning back across to the opposite lower back, hip and leg that is behind. Notice where you're able to lengthen across the front. Can you let your belly be soft and your chest to open?

Release – Slowly unwind your upper back to face forward, step forward with your leg that was behind so that your feet are parallel and let your arm rest down.

Rest – Notice where you have lengthened and softened across the back of the diagonal that you were just contracting.

Repeat a few times on the same side then take a walk and notice how coordinated your shoulder, arm, hip, and leg feel on this first side? Is it different to the other diagonal?

Repeat and compare with the other diagonal.

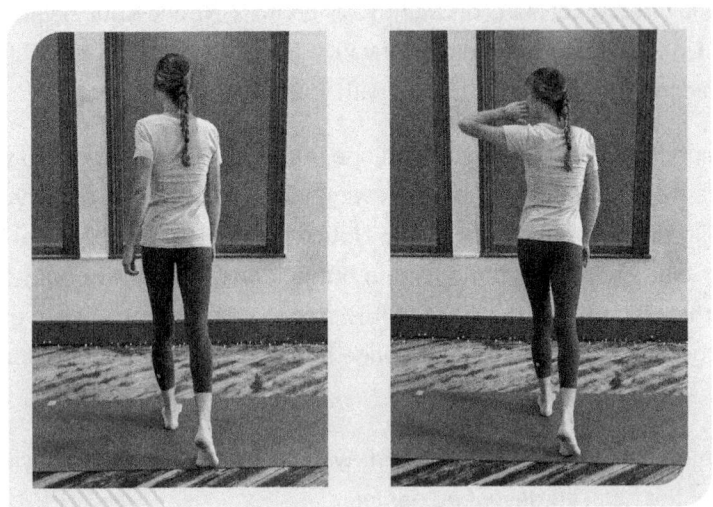

📝 NOTES & OBSERVATIONS

....

....

....

....

Hip Hikers

Reflex pattern – Trauma reflex

Helps to - Release one sided discomfort, pain and restricted movement espe-cially through the shoulders, pelvis, hips, knees and feet. Increases balance and equality of movement and function between left and right. Restores equal resting length through our waist. Enables freer vertical movement of the pelvis, essential for easy walking.

Bring your hands to the sides of your waist so that your fingertips point towards your navel and your thumbs point towards your lumbar spine. Notice the space between the sides of your ribcage and pelvis. Is the space and texture of your waist different between left and right? Choose a side to begin, then hike the side of your pelvis towards your waist in the direction of your armpit. Keep the same side leg straight and lift the heel as you hike the hip. You may feel that happening automatically because your leg and foot are connected to your waist. Notice how this leg 'appears' shorter.

Contract – Intentionally contract and shorten your waist under your hand as the hip hikes up, and feel how the opposite side of your waist lengthens.

Release – Begin to lengthen and make space at your waist as the hip lowers and the heel comes back down.

Rest – Notice the space between the side of your ribcage and pelvis.

Repeat this several times on each side and notice if you feel more weight through the lengthening side leg and foot as you hike? How does your head respond to this? You may notice it tipping slightly to the side that is hiking, because your head is connected to the muscles of your waist. If you don't notice this happening, explore how it feels to let it join in. Notice if this movement feels easier through one side.

NOTES & OBSERVATIONS

Reach for the top shelf

Thanks to Martha Peterson for creating and sharing this wonderful movement.

Reflex – Trauma

Helps to – Create balance through your sides and integrate your pandiculations into a full soma movement. It also helps you to more easily reach up high, such as to a high shelf, and restores the freedom of being able to use either hand to grab what you need!

Standing with your feet slightly wider than hip width and your arms up in a lazy Y position, begin to reach up with one arm as if you were reaching for something. Let your opposite heel lift up from the floor, hiking the hip towards your armpit as you do. Feel how your reaching side gently lengthens as the opposite side shortens.

Begin to release your hip hike, letting your heel lower as you do. As your reaching side returns to its resting length, begin to hike the hip as you now lift your heel and allow the other side to lengthen as you reach upwards with your other arm. Notice if it happens as freely on this side. How is your head involved in this pattern? If you were actually trying to grab something high up, you'd probably want to see if you're close to it, so let your head and gaze turn towards the hand that's reaching up.

Repeat from side to side. Can you explore this in a way that feels luxurious, as if you were just yawning your sides long, alternating shortening and lengthening through your sides.

As you come back to an equal length through your sides, allow your knees to soften and bend a little before switching your hip hike / reaching side. Allow your arms to rest down whenever you need.

NOTES & OBSERVATIONS

CHAPTER 13

Daily sequence: How to create a somatic movement habit

We are a process. We respond to life every single day. Our muscles are repeatedly contracting so that we can move, meet our needs, get things done, enjoy activities, play, and respond to stress. This is a continual process throughout our lives. Therefore, taking time to intentionally relax our muscles and reverse the accumulation of stress also needs to be a continual process. A regular practise is what creates the long-term changes in how we move and feel. The more you explore your somatic movement practise, the more profoundly you'll feel its effects. With a regular and effective practice, we're literally getting in the way of stress accumulating, becoming stuck and becoming normal. We are literally getting in the way of unnecessary and premature deterioration and decline. I like to compare the need for a daily practise to brushing your teeth. You wouldn't brush your teeth one day and then come back to them a week later for another clean. Well, at least not if you want to maintain healthy teeth and good breath! Nope, you'd brush your teeth twice a day. Head back to Chapter 6 for a reminder about habit building. There are plenty of books and ideas available about how to create new habits, one of which I've referenced throughout is James Clear's book *Atomic Habit*. If you're unsure where or how to begin, his 4 laws of creating behaviour change are a good starting point. Make it: Obvious, Attractive, Easy, and Satisfying. Notice how these qualities fit nicely with "how" we do our movement practise.

I like to use the analogy of map reading as another way of considering why we want to create a regular somatic movement practise. For those of you who, like me, love to venture off the beaten path, having the skills to use a compass and read a map are essential for your safety, wellbeing, and enjoyment of wandering over the hills and through the great outdoors.

Think of your sensory motor amnesia and any discomfort you may be experiencing as fog or unpleasant weather, where the path before you suddenly disappears from view. The more difficult the conditions, the more challenging it may be for you to keep moving forward and feel where you are not only in space, but also in relation to your own body; this is proprioception. If we only turn to our somatic practise when we begin to feel pain or discomfort, can it be as easy or effective if we haven't already rehearsed our ability to sense and relax our muscles under less difficult or painful conditions? Learning is easiest when we're not distracted by pain or stress. Imagine trying to learn and practise how to use a compass and read a map, only when your safety depends on it, when your footpath has disappeared, when you're already lost, tired, and cannot see where to go.

Like learning to map read and navigate in clear weather, how would practicing your somatic movements on the "clear sunny days" be even more effective for you, especially when we experience times of increased stress or discomfort? How would it be to repeat this practice until it becomes a skilful habit and your neurological pathways become so familiar that they can be sensed and controlled even when the "fog" of pain arrives? A bit like checking the weather forecast or practicing your skill of map reading before lacing up your walking boots and before you need to rely on your map-reading skills.

A regular practice of relieving the daily accumulation of muscle tension, not just when pain comes knocking, will help you to keep moving forward with more ease and less effort. This isn't about a "fix it" response to pain and discomfort when these sensations have stopped us in our tracks. This is about creating a lifestyle, a way of living in which we can continue to feel and live well. In my own practise, I've often found that the times I felt I didn't need it or had the time were when I needed it most.

Below are my top tips to help you create your own regular practice:

- Scans – no matter how much or little time you have for your practise, always take time for a soma scan.

- Attach your practise to something that you already do regularly, like brushing your teeth, getting ready for bed, or before and after an exercise that you do.
- Don't rush. If you're short on time, just explore one or two movements slowly and with awareness. One movement done intentionally will give you far more release than several repetitions that are rushed.
- Work with your environment. Do your practise where it's accessible, be that lying down, sitting, or standing.
- If your environment is noisy, pop on some headphones, noise cancelling if you have them, and close your eyes to help limit outside distractions.
- Mix up your practise. Whilst listening to what movements you feel you need in any given moment, ensure you add a variety of movements so that you're able to release and increase control of all muscle groups.

5-minute sequence

Soma scan
Arch and flatten
Soma scan

10-15-minute sequence

Soma scan
Arch and flatten
Baby back lift
Arch and curl
Soma scan

20-minute sequence

Soma scan
Arch and flatten
Rebalance the pelvis
Flower
Hip hikers
Soma scan

30-minute sequence

Soma scan
Arch and flatten
Arch and curl
Back lift
Diagonal arch and curl
Soma scan

 Some questions for you

- What daily routines do you have that you can attach some practise alongside?
- Where can you most easily and comfortably do your practise?
- When in your week can you commit to at least a few minutes to take a soma scan?
- When in your week can you commit to 5 minutes for a soma scan and arch and flatten?

CHAPTER SUMMARY

- ► Do it when you don't feel you need it.
- ► Don't wait for pain to come knocking.
- ► Make time for soma scans.
- ► Don't rush your practise. Fewer repetitions done somatically and with awareness is more effective than many repetitions done quickly without awareness.
- ► An effective practise doesn't have to be a long practise.
- ► Mix up your movements and practise habits.
- ► Create your practise habits by attaching it to something that you already do.

CHAPTER 14

Next steps: A future of unlimited potential, freedom, and autonomy

Find an Essential Somatics™ trained teacher.

As the number of teachers increases, this work will no doubt become more and more accessible to all of us. I look forward to the day when in-person classes are taking place in every town and city and are as available and easy to find as yoga and Pilates classes are. Perhaps you remember when that wasn't always the case. I cannot emphasise enough the importance and benefit of taking in-person classes with a trained teacher where you can be guided through your practise in person and receive direct hands-on guidance.

There is also great benefit in taking online classes too. Because CSE focuses upon sensing, awareness, and you making the changes yourself, it doesn't matter that you're in a different location to your teacher. After all, you're not trying to copy what you see someone / an instructor doing. You can just lie down and close your eyes, sending your awareness to your internal felt sense. Taking classes virtually provides a rich and regular experience for your practise. If I were to highlight one benefit that the pandemic has left us with, it's how normal and accessible taking online classes has become, even for those of us, myself included, who don't consider ourselves to be particularly tech savvy. The world is literally our oyster when it comes to finding the right teacher for us, regardless of where we are, providing the time zones work for us. It's always a pleasure to have somas join me in class from every corner of the globe, increasing connection near and far.

I like to think of joining a class as being like the main meal of my movement practise. Taking a class and being guided by a fellow teacher tops up and really nourishes the effects of my shorter daily practise. This isn't a case of choosing either or; both are necessary for creating and maintaining freedom.

Find an Essential Somatics™ Certified Clinical Somatic Educator (CCSE)

A clinical session is the most direct way of addressing your SMA habituated muscle tension that causes discomfort and restricted movement. The learning that takes place in tailored clinical sessions to address your specific needs is a rich experience. These sessions will go on to inform your own practise. Because clinical sessions aren't a treatment or intended to "fix" or "reset" you, they're not intended to be a regular long-term experience. You have the number of sessions ideal for you, then you move on to your own practice, including taking weekly movement classes.

Dive deeper

If you've experienced the changes that take place in just a short practise or 60-minute class, imagine the possibilities that await you by taking a deeper dive into your practise with day or weekend workshops and retreats. These are opportunities where you have more time to experience yourself in a different and deeper way, no matter how established a practise you have. There is *always* something to learn.

Training

For those of you who feel that itch to explore the possibility of teacher training, go ahead and dive deeply into your own practise. Your first-person experience is from where your understanding and your rich teaching will come, enabling you to guide others in the most effective ways. When I began to explore this method and my mind was blown, I had a deep need and desire to learn more, and I felt a knowing that, one day, I needed to teach it. Like many clients, and with equal amount of surprise and frustration, I found myself repeatedly asking, *"How do people not know about this?"* and *"Why have I not heard of this before?"*

How my life and that of those around me would have developed differently had I never stopped self-sensing, connecting, pandiculating, and being present to my needs.

A somatic centred approach to living

Let us share this work. If I may be so bold, join me in creating and remembering how to experience a somatic centred approach to living. Tell your friends, your family, your colleagues, your neighbour, people whom you don't yet know, the person next to you in a queue or on a plane or train. Together, we can help to enable and empower ourselves and each of our fellow somas. Together, we can build connections to ourselves and others, and we can be the free and autonomous beings we were designed to be. Every step towards a culture that reflects our true existence and essence of who and what we are begins with each of us. Awareness begins this process. We must first take time to become aware of where we are and be open to the idea that we know far less than we could; there is always something to notice; and there are always opportunities to learn, grow, and connect. Creating and maintaining long-term change and freedom for our living process requires intentional participation throughout our lives. A culture and society that reflects a somatic-centred approach to living is a future world I'll happily be a part of. This is a world I'll contentedly continue moving through with as much freedom and autonomy as possible, until my last breath. Won't you join me?

REFERENCES

Brown, Brené. *Daring Greatly: How the Courage to Be Vulnerable Transforms the Way We Live, Love, Parent and Lead.* Avery, 2015.

Calais-Germain, Blandine. *Anatomy of Movement.* Eastland Press, 2014.

Caldwell, Tommy. *The Push: A Climber's Search for the Path.* Penguin, 2018.

Clear, James. *Atomic Habits: An Easy & Proven Way to Build Good Habits & Break Bad Ones.* Random House Business, 2018.

Doidge, Norman. *The Brain That Changes Itself.* Penguin, 2008

Forencish, Frank. *Exuberant Animal: The Power of Health, Play and Joyful Movement.* Author House, 2006.

Francis, Gavin. *Recovery: The Lost Art of Convalescence.* Wellcome Collection, 2022.

Grant, Adam. *Think Again: The Power of Knowing What You Don't Know.* WH Allen, 2021.

Hanh, Thich Nhat. *Body and Mind Are One* (Audio CD). Sounds True, 2013.

Hanlon Johnson, Don. *Bone, Breath & Gesture.* North Atlantic Books, 1995.

Hanna, Thomas. *Bodies in Revolt: A Primer in Somatic Thinking.* Freeperson Press, 1970.

Hanna, Thomas. *Somatic Exercises for Full Breathing* (Audio CD). Somatic Systems Institute.

Hanna, Thomas. *Somatics: Reawakening the Mind's Control of Movement, Flexibility and Health*, Da Capo, 1988.

Hanna, Thomas. *The Body of Life: Creating New Pathways for Sensory Awareness and Fluid Movement.* Healing Arts Press, 1993.

Hanna, Thomas. *Wave One Lectures.* Somatics Educational Resources. Association for Hanna Somatic Education. 1990.

Hanna, Thomas. Audio Guides. Somatics Educational Resources. Association for Hanna Somatic Education.

Hanson, Rick and Richard Mendius. *Buddha's Brain: The Practical Neuroscience of Happiness, Love, and Wisdom*. New Harbinger, 2009.

Hersey, Tricia. *Rest Is Resistance: Free Yourself from Grind Culture and Reclaim Your Life*. Aster, 2022.

Hickok, Gregory. *The Myth of Mirror Neurons: The Real Neuroscience of Communication and Cognition*. W. W. Norton & Company, 2014.

Leslie, Ian. *Curious: The Desire to Know And Why Your Life Depends On It*. Quercus, 2015.

Maté, Gabor. *When the Body Says No: Exploring the Stress -Disease Connection*. Vermilion, 2019.

O'Sullivan, Suzanne. *It's All in Your Head: True Stories of Imaginary Illness*. Vintage, 2015.

Peterson, Martha. *Move Without Pain*. Sterling, 2011.

Rinpoche, Sogyal. *The Tibetan Book of Living and Dying*. Rider, 2002.

Rothschild, Babette. *The Body Remembers: The Psychophysiology of Trauma and Trauma Treatment*. W. W. Norton & Company, 2000.

Taylor, Daniel. *The Healing Power of Stories*. Doubleday, 1996.

Tucker, Louise. *An Introduction Guide to Anatomy and Physiology*. EMS Publishing, 2012

Van der Kolk, Bessel. *The Body Keeps the Score: Mind, Brain and Body in the Transformation of Trauma*. Penguin, 2014.

Useful resources

Websites

www.somatichabit.co.uk
www.essentialsomatics.com
https://www.associationforhannasomaticeducation.com/
www.ismeta.org

ACKNOWLEDGEMENTS

This book has been in my heart, soul, and mind for many years. Organising it into the format that you have before you has been a recent adventure, and one that has taken place during a time of momentous change in my life. Only through the support, belief, inspiration, and wisdom from others have I been able to make this happen. I will always be grateful and warmed by such connections to so many of you. You are all somewhere within these pages. Mel, you were the first person I told of my dream to write a book. From the start, your unwavering excitement, enthusiasm, and belief in my ability to do this, when I had none of my own, is at the core of what lies here before you. I feel you on every page. Martha, your vision for and evolution of Hanna's work, and your teachings, have changed my life. You've guided, held, nurtured, and supported me through so much of my somatic process, which has been messy and confusing at times, to say the least! I will always be indebted to you for seeing something within me that I could not quite see or access alone. I'm ever grateful for you guiding me towards not what to see, but where to look and explore. Your support with this project has undoubtedly benefited the quality upon these pages for all to digest, and to continue spreading this work with integrity. And to the rest of the Essential Somatics™ family, my international home, I thank you. Laura and Colm, how lucky I have been to have you as my mentors, receiving your ever generous support, knowledge, and wisdom. And to Rachel, for being by my side through our adventure together, and for our hours and hours of chats around all things somatics throughout and beyond our training. Those rich, deep, and often hilarious conversations and the thoughts and curiosity that they sparked are woven through these pages. To my parents and dearest friends, thank you. Whilst most of you had no idea that this project was taking place, your presence in my life has enabled me to indulge in and complete this book. I love you all and am deeply grateful for your continued love and support. Natalie Anne, thank you for inviting me to take that fateful ride with you, and sorry about scaring you with my flying through the air skills! I should probably also thank Chip, for knowing better than to let me attempt to control him. Adrian, thank you for seeing, hearing, and holding. Unconditional support and compassion are not always available or guaranteed, but, somehow, when I needed them most, I found you. The depth of this means more than I could possibly express here in words. To my fabulous book coaches Andrew and Allison, and the team at Self-Publishing School. Your enthusiasm for my project has been infectious throughout. Somehow, you all always had the right words, at the right time, when I didn't even know what I needed to hear to keep my vision moving forward. And to my editor, Wayne, I am so glad you have worked on this project with me. I am grateful for your clear support, guidance, and kindness through what felt like a daunting experience. Your skill, insights, and questions have evolved my rough draft towards the more polished product that I'd hoped it would become. I certainly could not have travelled there without your guidance. Lou, thank you for so warmly welcoming me into the York Pilates People family, and for providing a platform from which to share this work in our hometown of York. I am ever grateful for your and the YPP family's support. Tracy, thank you for continually helping me to move through my blockages to creating my dream. Your passion for my vision, support, and friendship, with your belief that anything we want we can achieve, has made so much possible for me with this work. Who knows, we might just fly... A big thank you to Alice Lodge Photography, for creating all of the images contained within this book. Alice, you are proof that everyone needs a friend who also happens to be an awesome photographer! Thank you for your love, care, and photography skills; I wouldn't have wanted anyone else behind the camera. Janet, thank you for giving me my first movement teacher opportunity and for bringing Thomas Hanna and Essential Somatics™ into my life. Life has never been the same since! And, finally, to every single client I've had the pleasure of working with and every single soma out there with whom I've talked about life and somatics, I give my never-ending gratitude. Thank you for showing up, thank you for your curiosity, and thank you for continually reminding me of how we can all benefit from this work. You never cease to humble and inspire me.

Thank you for reading my book!

Would you be able to take 2 minutes to leave me an honest review?

I need your input to make the next version of this
book and my future books even better and more helpful for my readers.

I really appreciate any feedback you can give and
look forward to hearing what you have to say.

Please take two minutes now to leave a helpful review on
Amazon letting me know what you thought of the book.

Thanks so much!
Karen

Printed in Great Britain
by Amazon

42483279R00086